Top Trends in
AI Self-Driving Cars

Practical Advances in Artificial Intelligence (AI)
and Machine Learning

Dr. Lance B. Eliot, MBA, PhD

Disclaimer: This book is presented solely for educational and entertainment purposes. The author and publisher are not offering it as legal, accounting, or other professional services advice. The author and publisher make no representations or warranties of any kind and assume no liabilities of any kind with respect to the accuracy or completeness of the contents and specifically disclaim any implied warranties of merchantability or fitness of use for a particular purpose. Neither the author nor the publisher shall be held liable or responsible to any person or entity with respect to any loss or incidental or consequential damages caused, or alleged to have been caused, directly or indirectly, by the information or programs contained herein. Every company is different and the advice and strategies contained herein may not be suitable for your situation.

DEDICATION

To my incredible son, Michael, and my incredible daughter, Lauren.

Forest fortuna adiuvat (from the Latin; good fortune favors the brave).

CONTENTS

Lance B. Eliot

ACKNOWLEDGMENTS

I have been the beneficiary of advice and counsel by many friends, colleagues, family, investors, and many others. I want to thank everyone that has aided me throughout my career. I write from the heart and the head, having experienced first-hand what it means to have others around you that support you during the good times and the tough times.

To Warren Bennis, one of my doctoral advisors and ultimately a colleague, I offer my deepest thanks and appreciation, especially for his calm and insightful wisdom and support.

To Mark Stevens and his generous efforts toward funding and supporting the USC Stevens Center for Innovation.

To Lloyd Greif and the USC Lloyd Greif Center for Entrepreneurial Studies for their ongoing encouragement of founders and entrepreneurs.

To Peter Drucker, William Wang, Aaron Levie, Peter Kim, Jon Kraft, Cindy Crawford, Jenny Ming, Steve Milligan, Chis Underwood, Frank Gehry, Buzz Aldrin, Steve Forbes, Bill Thompson, Dave Dillon, Alan Fuerstman, Larry Ellison, Jim Sinegal, John Sperling, Mark Stevenson, Anand Nallathambi, Thomas Barrack, Jr., and many other innovators and leaders that I have met and gained mightily from doing so.

Thanks to Ed Trainor, Kevin Anderson, James Hickey, Wendell Jones, Ken Harris, DuWayne Peterson, Mike Brown, Jim Thornton, Abhi Beniwal, Al Biland, John Nomura, Eliot Weinman, John Desmond, and many others for their unwavering support during my career.

And most of all thanks as always to Lauren and Michael, for their ongoing support and for having seen me writing and heard much of this material during the many months involved in writing it. To their patience and willingness to listen.

Lance B. Eliot

INTRODUCTION

This is a book that provides the newest innovations and the latest Artificial Intelligence (AI) advances about the emerging nature of AI-based autonomous self-driving driverless cars. Via recent advances in Artificial Intelligence (AI) and Machine Learning (ML), we are nearing the day when vehicles can control themselves and will not require and nor rely upon human intervention to perform their driving tasks (or, that <u>allow</u> for human intervention, but only *require* human intervention in very limited ways).

Similar to my other related books, which I describe in a moment and list the chapters in the Appendix A of this book, I am particularly focused on those advances that pertain to self-driving cars. The phrase "autonomous vehicles" is often used to refer to any kind of vehicle, whether it is ground-based or in the air or sea, and whether it is a cargo hauling trailer truck or a conventional passenger car. Though the aspects described in this book are certainly applicable to all kinds of autonomous vehicles, I am focused more so here on cars.

Indeed, I am especially known for my role in aiding the advancement of self-driving cars, serving currently as the Executive Director of the Cybernetic Self-Driving Cars Institute.. In addition to writing software, designing and developing systems and software for self-driving cars, I also speak and write quite a bit about the topic. This book is a collection of some of my more advanced essays. For those of you that might have seen my essays posted elsewhere, I have updated them and integrated them into this book as one handy cohesive package.

You might be interested in companion books that I have written that provide additional key innovations and fundamentals about self-driving cars. Those books are entitled **"Introduction to Driverless Self-Driving Cars,"** **"Advances in AI and Autonomous Vehicles: Cybernetic Self-Driving Cars,"** **"Self-Driving Cars: "The Mother of All AI Projects,"** **"Innovation and Thought Leadership on Self-Driving Driverless Cars,"** **"New Advances in AI Autonomous Driverless Self-Driving Cars,"** and **"Autonomous Vehicle Driverless Self-Driving Cars and**

Artificial Intelligence" and **"Transformative Artificial Intelligence Driverless Self-Driving Cars,"** and **"Disruptive Artificial Intelligence and Driverless Self-Driving Cars"** and **"State-of-the-Art AI Driverless Self-Driving Cars"** (they are all available via Amazon). See Appendix A of this herein book to see a listing of the chapters covered in those three books.

For the introduction here to this book, I am going to borrow my introduction from those companion books, since it does a good job of laying out the landscape of self-driving cars and my overall viewpoints on the topic. The remainder of the book is all new material that does not appear in the companion books.

INTRODUCTION TO SELF-DRIVING CARS

This is a book about self-driving cars. Someday in the future, we'll all have self-driving cars and this book will perhaps seem antiquated, but right now, we are at the forefront of the self-driving car wave. Daily news bombards us with flashes of new announcements by one car maker or another and leaves the impression that within the next few weeks or maybe months that the self-driving car will be here. A casual non-technical reader would assume from these news flashes that in fact we must be on the cusp of a true self-driving car.

Here's a real news flash: We are still quite a distance from having a true self-driving car. It is years to go before we get there.

Why is that? Because a true self-driving car is akin to a moonshot. In the same manner that getting us to the moon was an incredible feat, likewise can it be said for achieving a true self-driving car. Anybody that suggests or even brashly states that the true self-driving car is nearly here should be viewed with great skepticism. Indeed, you'll see that I often tend to use the word "hogwash" or "crock" when I assess much of the decidedly *fake news* about self-driving cars. Those of us on the inside know that what is often reported to the outside is malarkey. Few of the insiders are willing to say so. I have no such hesitation.

Indeed, I've been writing a popular blog post about self-driving cars and hitting hard on those that try to wave their hands and pretend that we are on the imminent verge of true self-driving cars. For many years, I've been known as the AI Insider. Besides writing about AI, I also develop AI software. I do what I describe. It also gives me insights into what others that are doing AI are really doing versus what it is said they are doing.

Many faithful readers had asked me to pull together my insightful short essays and put them into another book, which you are now holding in your hands.

For those of you that have been reading my essays over the years, this collection not only puts them together into one handy package, I also updated the essays and added new material. For those of you that are new to the topic of self-driving cars and AI, I hope you find these essays approachable and informative. I also tend to have a writing style with a bit of a voice, and so you'll see that I am times have a wry sense of humor and also like to poke at conformity.

As a former professor and founder of an AI research lab, I for many years wrote in the formal language of academic writing. I published in referred journals and served as an editor for several AI journals. This writing here is not of the nature, and I have adopted a different and more informal style for these essays. That being said, I also do mention from time-to-time more rigorous material on AI and encourage you all to dig into those deeper and more formal materials if so interested.

I am also an AI practitioner. This means that I write AI software for a living. Currently, I head-up the Cybernetics Self-Driving Car Institute, where we are developing AI software for self-driving cars. I am excited to also report that my son, also a software engineer, heads-up our Cybernetics Self-Driving Car Lab. What I have helped to start, and for which he is an integral part, ultimately he will carry long into the future after I have retired. My daughter, a marketing whiz, also is integral to our efforts as head of our Marketing group. She too will carry forward the legacy now being formulated.

For those of you that are reading this book and have a penchant for writing code, you might consider taking a look at the open source code available for self-driving cars. This is a handy place to start learning how to develop AI for self-driving cars. There are also many new educational courses spring forth.

There is a growing body of those wanting to learn about and develop self-driving cars, and a growing body of colleges, labs, and other avenues by which you can learn about self-driving cars.

This book will provide a foundation of aspects that I think will get you ready for those kinds of more advanced training opportunities. If you've already taken those classes, you'll likely find these essays especially interesting as they offer a perspective that I am betting few other instructors or faculty offered to you. These are challenging essays that ask you to think beyond the conventional about self-driving cars.

THE MOTHER OF ALL AI PROJECTS

In June 2017, Apple CEO Tim Cook came out and finally admitted that Apple has been working on a self-driving car. As you'll see in my essays, Apple was enmeshed in secrecy about their self-driving car efforts. We have only been able to read the tea leaves and guess at what Apple has been up to. The notion of an iCar has been floating for quite a while, and self-driving engineers and researchers have been signing tight-lipped Non-Disclosure Agreements (NDA's) to work on projects at Apple that were as shrouded in mystery as any military invasion plans might be.

Tim Cook said something that many others in the Artificial Intelligence (AI) field have been saying, namely, the creation of a self-driving car has got to be the mother of all AI projects. In other words, it is in fact a tremendous moonshot for AI. If a self-driving car can be crafted and the AI works as we hope, it means that we have made incredible strides with AI and that therefore it opens many other worlds of potential breakthrough accomplishments that AI can solve.

Is this hyperbole? Am I just trying to make AI seem like a miracle worker and so provide self-aggrandizing statements for those of us writing the AI software for self-driving cars? No, it is not hyperbole. Developing a true self-driving car is really, really, really hard to do. Let me take a moment to explain why. As a side note, I realize that the Apple CEO is known for at times uttering hyperbole, and he had previously said for example that the year 2012 was "the mother of all years," and he had said that the release of iOS 10 was "the mother of all releases" – all of which does suggest he likes to use the handy "mother of" expression. But, I assure you, in terms of true self-driving cars, he has hit the nail on the head. For sure.

When you think about a moonshot and how we got to the moon, there are some identifiable characteristics and those same aspects can be applied to creating a true self-driving car. You'll notice that I keep putting the word "true" in front of the self-driving car expression. I do so because as per my essay about the various levels of self-driving cars, there are some self-driving cars that are only somewhat of a self-driving car. The somewhat versions are ones that require a human driver to be ready to intervene. In my view, that's not a true self-driving car. A true self-driving car is one that requires no human driver intervention at all. It is a car that can entirely undertake via automation the driving task without any human driver needed. This is the essence of what is known as a Level 5 self-driving car. We are currently at the Level 2 and Level 3 mark, and not yet at Level 5.

Getting to the moon involved aspects such as having big stretch goals, incremental progress, experimentation, innovation, and so on. Let's review how this applied to the moonshot of the bygone era, and how it applies to the self-driving car moonshot of today.

Big Stretch Goal

Trying to take a human and deliver the human to the moon, and bring them back, safely, was an extremely large stretch goal at the time. No one knew whether it could be done. The technology wasn't available yet. The cost was huge. The determination would need to be fierce. Etc. To reach a Level 5 self-driving car is going to be the same. It is a big stretch goal. We can readily get to the Level 3, and we are able to see the Level 4 just up ahead, but a Level 5 is still an unknown as to if it is doable. It should eventually be doable and in the same way that we thought we'd eventually get to the moon, but when it will occur is a different story.

Incremental Progress

Getting to the moon did not happen overnight in one fell swoop. It took years and years of incremental progress to get there. Likewise for self-driving cars. Google has famously been striving to get to the Level 5, and pretty much been willing to forgo dealing with the intervening levels, but most of the other self-driving car makers are doing the incremental route. Let's get a good Level 2 and a somewhat Level 3 going. Then, let's improve the Level 3 and get a somewhat Level 4 going. Then, let's improve the Level 4 and finally arrive at a Level 5. This seems to be the prevalent way that we are going to achieve the true self-driving car.

Experimentation

You likely know that there were various experiments involved in perfecting the approach and technology to get to the moon. As per making incremental progress, we first tried to see if we could get a rocket to go into space and safety return, then put a monkey in there, then with a human, then we went all the way to the moon but didn't land, and finally we arrived at the mission that actually landed on the moon. Self-driving cars are the same way. We are doing simulations of self-driving cars. We do testing of self-driving cars on private land under controlled situations. We do testing of self-driving cars on public roadways, often having to meet regulatory requirements including for example having an engineer or equivalent in the car to take over the controls if needed. And so on. Experiments big and small are needed to figure out what works and what doesn't.

Innovation

There are already some advances in AI that are allowing us to progress toward self-driving cars. We are going to need even more advances. Innovation in all aspects of technology are going to be required to achieve a true self-driving car. By no means do we already have everything in-hand that we need to get there. Expect new inventions and new approaches, new algorithms, etc.

Setbacks

Most of the pundits are avoiding talking about potential setbacks in the progress toward self-driving cars. Getting to the moon involved many setbacks, some of which you never have heard of and were buried at the time so as to not dampen enthusiasm and funding for getting to the moon. A recurring theme in many of my included essays is that there are going to be setbacks as we try to arrive at a true self-driving car. Take a deep breath and be ready. I just hope the setbacks don't completely stop progress. I am sure that it will cause progress to alter in a manner that we've not yet seen in the self-driving car field. I liken the self-driving car of today to the excitement everyone had for Uber when it first got going. Today, we have a different view of Uber and with each passing day there are more regulations to the ride sharing business and more concerns raised. The darling child only stays a darling until finally that child acts up. It will happen the same with self-driving cars.

SELF-DRIVING CARS CHALLENGES

But what exactly makes things so hard to have a true self-driving car, you might be asking. You have seen cruise control for years and years. You've lately seen cars that can do parallel parking. You've seen YouTube videos of Tesla drivers that put their hands out the window as their car zooms along the highway, and seen to therefore be in a self-driving car. Aren't we just needing to put a few more sensors onto a car and then we'll have in-hand a true self-driving car? Nope.

Consider for a moment the nature of the driving task. We don't just let anyone at any age drive a car. Worldwide, most countries won't license a driver until the age of 18, though many do allow a learner's permit at the age of 15 or 16. Some suggest that a younger age would be physically too small to reach the controls of the car. Though this might be the case, we could easily adjust the controls to allow for younger aged and thus smaller stature. It's not their physical size that matters. It's their cognitive development that matters.

To drive a car, you need to be able to reason about the car, what the car can and cannot do. You need to know how to operate the car. You need to know about how other cars on the road drive. You need to know what is allowed in driving such as speed limits and driving within marked lanes. You need to be able to react to situations and be able to avoid getting into accidents. You need to ascertain when to hit your brakes, when to steer clear of a pedestrian, and how to keep from ramming that motorcyclist that just cut you off.

Many of us had taken courses on driving. We studied about driving and took driver training. We had to take a test and pass it to be able to drive. The point being that though most adults take the driving task for granted, and we often "mindlessly" drive our cars, there is a significant amount of cognitive effort that goes into driving a car. After a while, it becomes second nature. You don't especially think about how you drive, you just do it. But, if you watch a novice driver, say a teenager learning to drive, you suddenly realize that there is a lot more complexity to it than we seem to realize.

Furthermore, driving is a very serious task. I recall when my daughter and son first learned to drive. They are both very conscientious people. They wanted to make sure that whatever they did, they did well, and that they did not harm anyone. Every day, when you get into a car, it is probably around 4,000 pounds of hefty metal and plastics (about two tons), and it is a lethal weapon. Think about it. You drive down the street in an object that weighs two tons and with the engine it can accelerate and ram into anything you want to hit. The damage a car can inflict is very scary. Both my children were surprised that they were being given the right to maneuver this monster of a beast that could cause tremendous harm entirely by merely letting go of the steering wheel for a moment or taking your eyes off the road.

In fact, in the United States alone there are about 30,000 deaths per year by auto accidents, which is around 100 per day. Given that there are about 263 million cars in the United States, I am actually more amazed that the number of fatalities is not a lot higher. During my morning commute, I look at all the thousands of cars on the freeway around me, and I think that if all of them decided to go zombie and drive in a crazy maniac way, there would be many people dead. Somehow, incredibly, each day, most people drive relatively safely. To me, that's a miracle right there. Getting millions and millions of people to be safe and sane when behind the wheel of a two ton mobile object, it's a feat that we as a society should admire with pride.

So, hopefully you are in agreement that the driving task requires a great deal of cognition. You don't' need to be especially smart to drive a car, and we've done quite a bit to make car driving viable for even the average dolt. There isn't an IQ test that you need to take to drive a car. If you can read and write, and pass a test, you pretty much can legally drive a car. There are of course some that drive a car and are not legally permitted to do so, plus there are private areas such as farms where drivers are young, but for public roadways in the United States, you can be generally of average intelligence (or less) and be able to legally drive.

This though makes it seem like the cognitive effort must not be much. If the cognitive effort was truly hard, wouldn't we only have Einstein's that could drive a car? We have made sure to keep the driving task as simple as we can, by making the controls easy and relatively standardized, and by having roads that are relatively standardized, and so on. It is as though Disneyland has put their Autopia into the real-world, by us all as a society agreeing that roads will be a certain way, and we'll all abide by the various rules of driving.

A modest cognitive task by a human is still something that stymies AI. You certainly know that AI has been able to beat chess players and be good at other kinds of games. This type of narrow cognition is not what car driving is about. Car driving is much wider. It requires knowledge about the world, which a chess playing AI system does not need to know. The cognitive aspects of driving are on the one hand seemingly simple, but at the same time require layer upon layer of knowledge about cars, people, roads, rules, and a myriad of other "common sense" aspects. We don't have any AI systems today that have that same kind of breadth and depth of awareness and knowledge.

As revealed in my essays, the self-driving car of today is using trickery to do particular tasks. It is all very narrow in operation. Plus, it currently assumes that a human driver is ready to intervene. It is like a child that we have taught to stack blocks, but we are needed to be right there in case the child stacks them too high and they begin to fall over. AI of today is brittle, it is narrow, and it does not approach the cognitive abilities of humans. This is why the true self-driving car is somewhere out in the future.

Another aspect to the driving task is that it is not solely a mind exercise. You do need to use your senses to drive. You use your eyes a vision sensors to see the road ahead. You vision capability is like a streaming video, which your brain needs to continually analyze as you drive. Where is the road? Is there a pedestrian in the way? Is there another car ahead of you? Your senses are relying a flood of info to your brain. Self-driving cars are trying to do the same, by using cameras, radar, ultrasound, and lasers. This is an attempt at mimicking how humans have senses and sensory apparatus.

Thus, the driving task is mental and physical. You use your senses, you use your arms and legs to manipulate the controls of the car, and you use your brain to assess the sensory info and direct your limbs to act upon the controls of the car. This all happens instantly. If you've ever perhaps gotten something in your eye and only had one eye available to drive with, you suddenly realize how dependent upon vision you are. If you have a broken foot with a cast, you suddenly realize how hard it is to control the brake pedal and the accelerator. If you've taken medication and your brain is maybe sluggish, you suddenly realize how much mental strain is required to drive a car.

An AI system that plays chess only needs to be focused on playing chess. The physical aspects aren't important because usually a human moves the chess pieces or the chessboard is shown on an electronic display. Using AI for a more life-and-death task such as analyzing MRI images of patients, this again does not require physical capabilities and instead is done by examining images of bits.

Driving a car is a true life-and-death task. It is a use of AI that can easily and at any moment produce death. For those colleagues of mine that are developing this AI, as am I, we need to keep in mind the somber aspects of this. We are producing software that will have in its virtual hands the lives of the occupants of the car, and the lives of those in other nearby cars, and the lives of nearby pedestrians, etc. Chess is not usually a life-or-death matter.

Driving is all around us. Cars are everywhere. Most of today's AI applications involve only a small number of people. Or, they are behind the scenes and we as humans have other recourse if the AI messes up. AI that is driving a car at 80 miles per hour on a highway had better not mess up. The consequences are grave. Multiply this by the number of cars, if we could put magically self-driving into every car in the USA, we'd have AI running in the 263 million cars. That's a lot of AI spread around. This is AI on a massive scale that we are not doing today and that offers both promise and potential peril.

There are some that want AI for self-driving cars because they envision a world without any car accidents. They envision a world in which there is no car congestion and all cars cooperate with each other. These are wonderful utopian visions.

They are also very misleading. The adoption of self-driving cars is going to be incremental and not overnight. We cannot economically just junk all existing cars. Nor are we going to be able to affordably retrofit existing cars. It is more likely that self-driving cars will be built into new cars and that over many years of gradual replacement of existing cars that we'll see the mix of self-driving cars become substantial in the real-world.

In these essays, I have tried to offer technological insights without being overly technical in my description, and also blended the business, societal, and economic aspects too. Technologists need to consider the non-technological impacts of what they do. Non-technologists should be aware of what is being developed.

We all need to work together to collectively be prepared for the enormous disruption and transformative aspects of true self-driving cars. We all need to be involved in this mother of all AI projects.

WHAT THIS BOOK PROVIDES

What does this book provide to you? It introduces many of the key elements about self-driving cars and does so with an AI based perspective. I weave together technical and non-technical aspects, readily going from being concerned about the cognitive capabilities of the driving task and how the technology is embodying this into self-driving cars, and in the next breath I discuss the societal and economic aspects.

They are all intertwined because that's the way reality is. You cannot separate out the technology per se, and instead must consider it within the milieu of what is being invented and innovated, and do so with a mindset towards the contemporary mores and culture that shape what we are doing and what we hope to do.

WHY THIS BOOK

I wrote this book to try and bring to the public view many aspects about self-driving cars that nobody seems to be discussing.

For business leaders that are either involved in making self-driving cars or that are going to leverage self-driving cars, I hope that this book will enlighten you as to the risks involved and ways in which you should be strategizing about how to deal with those risks.

For entrepreneurs, startups and other businesses that want to enter into the self-driving car market that is emerging, I hope this book sparks your interest in doing so, and provides some sense of what might be prudent to pursue.

For researchers that study self-driving cars, I hope this book spurs your interest in the risks and safety issues of self-driving cars, and also nudges you toward conducting research on those aspects.

For students in computer science or related disciplines, I hope this book will provide you with interesting and new ideas and material, for which you might conduct research or provide some career direction insights for you.

For AI companies and high-tech companies pursuing self-driving cars, this book will hopefully broaden your view beyond just the mere coding and development needed to make self-driving cars.

For all readers, I hope that you will find the material in this book to be stimulating. Some of it will be repetitive of things you already know. But I am pretty sure that you'll also find various eureka moments whereby you'll discover a new technique or approach that you had not earlier thought of. I am also betting that there will be material that forces you to rethink some of your current practices.

I am not saying you will suddenly have an epiphany and change what you are doing. I do think though that you will reconsider or perhaps revisit what you are doing.

For anyone choosing to use this book for teaching purposes, please take a look at my suggestions for doing so, as described in the Appendix. I have found the material handy in courses that I have taught, and likewise other faculty have told me that they have found the material handy, in some cases as extended readings and in other instances as a core part of their course (depending on the nature of the class).

In my writing for this book, I have tried carefully to blend both the practitioner and the academic styles of writing. It is not as dense as is typical academic journal writing, but at the same time offers depth by going into the nuances and trade-offs of various practices.

The word "deep" is in vogue today, meaning getting deeply into a subject or topic, and so is the word "unpack" which means to tease out the underlying aspects of a subject or topic. I have sought to offer material that addresses an issue or topic by going relatively deeply into it and make sure that it is well unpacked.

Finally, in any book about AI, it is difficult to use our everyday words without having some of them be misinterpreted. Specifically, it is easy to anthropomorphize AI. When I say that an AI system "knows" something, I do not want you to construe that the AI system has sentience and "knows" in the same way that humans do. They aren't that way, as yet. I have tried to use quotes around such words from time-to-time to emphasize that the words I am using should not be misinterpreted to ascribe true human intelligence to the AI systems that we know of today. If I used quotes around all such words, the book would be very difficult to read, and so I am doing so judiciously. Please keep that in mind as you read the material, thanks.

Lance B. Eliot

COMPANION BOOKS

If you find this material of interest, you might want to also see my other books on self-driving cars, entitled:

1. **"Introduction to Driverless Self-Driving Cars"** by Dr. Lance Eliot

2. **"Innovation and Thought Leadership on Self-Driving Driverless Cars"** by Dr. Lance Eliot

3. **"Advances in AI and Autonomous Vehicles: Cybernetic Self-Driving Cars"** by Dr. Lance Eliot

4. *"Self-Driving Cars: The Mother of All AI Projects"* by Dr. Lance Eliot

5. **"New Advances in AI Autonomous Driverless Self-Driving Cars"** by Dr. Lance Eliot

6. **"Autonomous Vehicle Driverless Self-Driving Cars and Artificial Intelligence"** by Dr. Lance Eliot and Michael B. Eliot

7. **"Transformative Artificial Intelligence Driverless Self-Driving Cars"** by Dr. Lance Eliot

8. **"Disruptive Artificial Intelligence and Driverless Self-Driving Cars"** by Dr. Lance Eliot

9. "State-of-the-Art AI Driverless Self-Driving Cars" by Dr. Lance Eliot

10. **"Top Trends in AI Self-Driving Cars"** by Dr. Lance Eliot

All of the above books are available on Amazon and at other major global booksellers.

Lance B. Eliot

CHAPTER 1

ELIOT FRAMEWORK FOR AI SELF-DRIVING CARS

Lance B. Eliot

CHAPTER 1

ELIOT FRAMEWORK FOR AI SELF-DRIVING CARS

This chapter is a core foundational aspect for understanding AI self-driving cars and I have used this same chapter in several of my other books to introduce the reader to essential elements of this field. Once you've read this chapter, you'll be prepared to read the rest of the material since the foundational essence of the components of autonomous AI driverless self-driving cars will have been established for you.

When I give presentations about self-driving cars and teach classes on the topic, I have found it helpful to provide a framework around which the various key elements of self-driving cars can be understood and organized (see diagram at the end of this chapter). The framework needs to be simple enough to convey the overarching elements, but at the same time not so simple that it belies the true complexity of self-driving cars. As such, I am going to describe the framework here and try to offer in a thousand words (or more!) what the framework diagram itself intends to portray.

The core elements on the diagram are numbered for ease of reference. The numbering does not suggest any kind of prioritization of the elements. Each element is crucial. Each element has a purpose, and otherwise would not be included in the framework. For some self-driving cars, a particular element might be more important or somehow distinguished in comparison to other self-driving cars.

You could even use the framework to rate a particular self-driving car, doing so by gauging how well it performs in each of the elements of the framework. I will describe each of the elements, one at a time. After doing so, I'll discuss aspects that illustrate how the elements interact and perform during the overall effort of a self-driving car.

At the Cybernetic Self-Driving Car Institute, we use the framework to keep track of what we are working on, and how we are developing software that fills in what is needed to achieve Level 5 self-driving cars.

D-01: Sensor Capture

Let's start with the one element that often gets the most attention in the press about self-driving cars, namely, the sensory devices for a self-driving car.

On the framework, the box labeled as D-01 indicates "Sensor Capture" and refers to the processes of the self-driving car that involve collecting data from the myriad of sensors that are used for a self-driving car. The types of devices typically involved are listed, such as the use of mono cameras, stereo cameras, LIDAR devices, radar systems, ultrasonic devices, GPS, IMU, and so on.

These devices are tasked with obtaining data about the status of the self-driving car and the world around it. Some of the devices are continually providing updates, while others of the devices await an indication by the self-driving car that the device is supposed to collect data. The data might be first transformed in some fashion by the device itself, or it might instead be fed directly into the sensor capture as raw data. At that point, it might be up to the sensor capture processes to do transformations on the data. This all varies depending upon the nature of the devices being used and how the devices were designed and developed.

D-02: Sensor Fusion

Imagine that your eyeballs receive visual images, your nose receives odors, your ears receive sounds, and in essence each of your distinct sensory devices is getting some form of input. The input befits the nature of the device. Likewise, for a self-driving car, the cameras provide visual images, the radar returns radar reflections, and so on.

Each device provides the data as befits what the device does.

At some point, using the analogy to humans, you need to merge together what your eyes see, what your nose smells, what your ears hear, and piece it all together into a larger sense of what the world is all about and what is happening around you. Sensor fusion is the action of taking the singular aspects from each of the devices and putting them together into a larger puzzle.

Sensor fusion is a tough task. There are some devices that might not be working at the time of the sensor capture. Or, there might some devices that are unable to report well what they have detected. Again, using a human analogy, suppose you are in a dark room and so your eyes cannot see much. At that point, you might need to rely more so on your ears and what you hear. The same is true for a self-driving car. If the cameras are obscured due to snow and sleet, it might be that the radar can provide a greater indication of what the external conditions consist of.

In the case of a self-driving car, there can be a plethora of such sensory devices. Each is reporting what it can. Each might have its difficulties. Each might have its limitations, such as how far ahead it can detect an object. All of these limitations need to be considered during the sensor fusion task.

D-03: Virtual World Model

For humans, we presumably keep in our minds a model of the world around us when we are driving a car. In your mind, you know that the car is going at say 60 miles per hour and that you are on a freeway. You have a model in your mind that your car is surrounded by other cars, and that there are lanes to the freeway. Your model is not only based on what you can see, hear, etc., but also what you know about the nature of the world. You know that at any moment that car ahead of you can smash on its brakes, or the car behind you can ram into your car, or that the truck in the next lane might swerve into your lane.

The AI of the self-driving car needs to have a virtual world model, which it then keeps updated with whatever it is receiving from the sensor fusion, which received its input from the sensor capture and the sensory devices.

D-04: System Action Plan

By having a virtual world model, the AI of the self-driving car is able to keep track of where the car is and what is happening around the car. In addition, the AI needs to determine what to do next. Should the self-driving car hit its brakes? Should the self-driving car stay in its lane or swerve into the lane to the left? Should the self-driving car accelerate or slow down?

A system action plan needs to be prepared by the AI of the self-driving car. The action plan specifies what actions should be taken. The actions need to pertain to the status of the virtual world model. Plus, the actions need to be realizable.

This realizability means that the AI cannot just assert that the self-driving car should suddenly sprout wings and fly. Instead, the AI must be bound by whatever the self-driving car can actually do, such as coming to a halt in a distance of X feet at a speed of Y miles per hour, rather than perhaps asserting that the self-driving car come to a halt in 0 feet as though it could instantaneously come to a stop while it is in motion.

D-05: Controls Activation

The system action plan is implemented by activating the controls of the car to act according to what the plan stipulates. This might mean that the accelerator control is commanded to increase the speed of the car. Or, the steering control is commanded to turn the steering wheel 30 degrees to the left or right.

One question arises as to whether or not the controls respond as they are commanded to do. In other words, suppose the AI has commanded the accelerator to increase, but for some reason it does not do so. Or, maybe it tries to do so, but the speed of the car does not increase. The controls activation feeds back into the virtual world model, and simultaneously the virtual world model is getting updated from the sensors, the sensor capture, and the sensor fusion. This allows the AI to ascertain what has taken place as a result of the controls being commanded to take some kind of action.

By the way, please keep in mind that though the diagram seems to have a linear progression to it, the reality is that these are all aspects of the self-driving car that are happening in parallel and simultaneously. The sensors are capturing data, meanwhile the sensor fusion is taking place, meanwhile the virtual model is being updated, meanwhile the system action plan is being formulated and reformulated, meanwhile the controls are being activated.

This is the same as a human being that is driving a car. They are eyeballing the road, meanwhile they are fusing in their mind the sights, sounds, etc., meanwhile their mind is updating their model of the world around them, meanwhile they are formulating an action plan of what to do, and meanwhile they are pushing their foot onto the pedals and steering the car. In the normal course of driving a car, you are doing all of these at once. I mention this so that when you look at the diagram, you will think of the boxes as processes that are all happening at the same time, and not as though only one happens and then the next.

They are shown diagrammatically in a simplistic manner to help comprehend what is taking place. You though should also realize that they are working in parallel and simultaneous with each other. This is a tough aspect in that the inter-element communications involve latency and other aspects that must be taken into account. There can be delays in one element updating and then sharing its latest status with other elements.

D-06: Automobile & CAN

Contemporary cars use various automotive electronics and a Controller Area Network (CAN) to serve as the components that underlie the driving aspects of a car. There are Electronic Control Units (ECU's) which control subsystems of the car, such as the engine, the brakes, the doors, the windows, and so on.

The elements D-01, D-02, D-03, D-04, D-05 are layered on top of the D-06, and must be aware of the nature of what the D-06 is able to do and not do.

D-07: In-Car Commands

Humans are going to be occupants in self-driving cars. In a Level 5 self-driving car, there must be some form of communication that takes place between the humans and the self-driving car. For example, I go into a self-driving car and tell it that I want to be driven over to Disneyland, and along the way I want to stop at In-and-Out Burger. The self-driving car now parses what I've said and tries to then establish a means to carry out my wishes.

In-car commands can happen at any time during a driving journey. Though my example was about an in-car command when I first got into my self-driving car, it could be that while the self-driving car is carrying out the journey that I change my mind. Perhaps after getting stuck in traffic, I tell the self-driving car to forget about getting the burgers and just head straight over to the theme park. The self-driving car needs to be alert to in-car commands throughout the journey.

D-08: VX2 Communications

We will ultimately have self-driving cars communicating with each other, doing so via V2V (Vehicle-to-Vehicle) communications. We will also have self-driving cars that communicate with the roadways and other aspects of the transportation infrastructure, doing so via V2I (Vehicle-to-Infrastructure).

The variety of ways in which a self-driving car will be communicating with other cars and infrastructure is being called V2X, whereby the letter X means whatever else we identify as something that a car should or would want to communicate with. The V2X communications will be taking place simultaneous with everything else on the diagram, and those other elements will need to incorporate whatever it gleans from those V2X communications.

D-09: Deep Learning

The use of Deep Learning permeates all other aspects of the self-driving car. The AI of the self-driving car will be using deep learning to do a better job at the systems action plan, and at the controls activation, and at the sensor fusion, and so on.

Currently, the use of artificial neural networks is the most prevalent form of deep learning. Based on large swaths of data, the neural networks attempt to "learn" from the data and therefore direct the efforts of the self-driving car accordingly.

D-10: Tactical AI

Tactical AI is the element of dealing with the moment-to-moment driving of the self-driving car. Is the self-driving car staying in its lane of the freeway? Is the car responding appropriately to the controls commands? Are the sensory devices working?

For human drivers, the tactical equivalent can be seen when you watch a novice driver such as a teenager that is first driving. They are focused on the mechanics of the driving task, keeping their eye on the road while also trying to properly control the car.

D-11: Strategic AI

The Strategic AI aspects of a self-driving car are dealing with the larger picture of what the self-driving car is trying to do. If I had asked that the self-driving car take me to Disneyland, there is an overall journey map that needs to be kept and maintained.

There is an interaction between the Strategic AI and the Tactical AI. The Strategic AI is wanting to keep on the mission of the driving, while the Tactical AI is focused on the particulars underway in the driving effort. If the Tactical AI seems to wander away from the overarching mission, the Strategic AI wants to see why and get things back on track. If the Tactical AI realizes that there is something amiss on the self-driving car, it needs to alert the Strategic AI accordingly and have an adjustment to the overarching mission that is underway.

D-12: Self-Aware AI

Very few of the self-driving cars being developed are including a Self-Aware AI element, which we at the Cybernetic Self-Driving Car Institute believe is crucial to Level 5 self-driving cars.

The Self-Aware AI element is intended to watch over itself, in the sense that the AI is making sure that the AI is working as intended. Suppose you had a human driving a car, and they were starting to drive erratically. Hopefully, their own self-awareness would make them realize they themselves are driving poorly, such as perhaps starting to fall asleep after having been driving for hours on end. If you had a passenger in the car, they might be able to alert the driver if the driver is starting to do something amiss. This is exactly what the Self-Aware

AI element tries to do, it becomes the overseer of the AI, and tries to detect when the AI has become faulty or confused, and then find ways to overcome the issue.

D-13: Economic

The economic aspects of a self-driving car are not per se a technology aspect of a self-driving car, but the economics do indeed impact the nature of a self-driving car. For example, the cost of outfitting a self-driving car with every kind of possible sensory device is prohibitive, and so choices need to be made about which devices are used. And, for those sensory devices chosen, whether they would have a full set of features or a more limited set of features.

We are going to have self-driving cars that are at the low-end of a consumer cost point, and others at the high-end of a consumer cost point. You cannot expect that the self-driving car at the low-end is going to be as robust as the one at the high-end. I realize that many of the self-driving car pundits are acting as though all self-driving cars will be the same, but they won't be. Just like anything else, we are going to have self-driving cars that have a range of capabilities. Some will be better than others. Some will be safer than others. This is the way of the real-world, and so we need to be thinking about the economics aspects when considering the nature of self-driving cars.

D-14: Societal

This component encompasses the societal aspects of AI which also impacts the technology of self-driving cars. For example, the famous Trolley Problem involves what choices should a self-driving car make when faced with life-and-death matters. If the self-driving car is about to either hit a child standing in the roadway, or instead ram into a tree at the side of the road and possibly kill the humans in the self-driving car, which choice should be made?

We need to keep in mind the societal aspects will underlie the AI of the self-driving car. Whether we are aware of it explicitly or not, the AI will have embedded into it various societal assumptions.

D-15: Innovation

I included the notion of innovation into the framework because we can anticipate that whatever a self-driving car consists of, it will continue to be innovated over time. The self-driving cars coming out in the next several years will undoubtedly be different and less innovative than the versions that come out in ten years hence, and so on.

Framework Overall

For those of you that want to learn about self-driving cars, you can potentially pick a particular element and become specialized in that aspect. Some engineers are focusing on the sensory devices. Some engineers focus on the controls activation. And so on. There are specialties in each of the elements.

Researchers are likewise specializing in various aspects. For example, there are researchers that are using Deep Learning to see how best it can be used for sensor fusion. There are other researchers that are using Deep Learning to derive good System Action Plans. Some are studying how to develop AI for the Strategic aspects of the driving task, while others are focused on the Tactical aspects.

A well-prepared all-around software developer that is involved in self-driving cars should be familiar with all of the elements, at least to the degree that they know what each element does. This is important since whatever piece of the pie that the software developer works on, they need to be knowledgeable about what the other elements are doing.

Lance B. Eliot

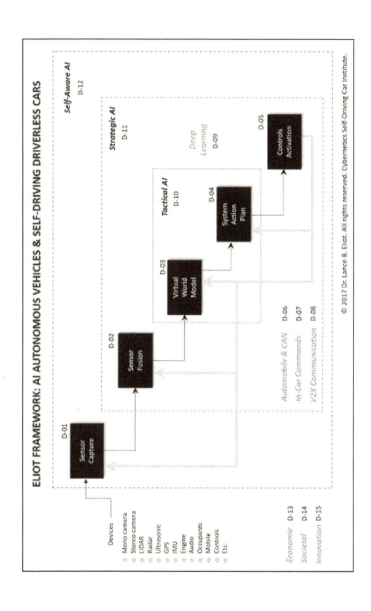

ELIOT FRAMEWORK: AI AUTONOMOUS VEHICLES & SELF-DRIVING DRIVERLESS CARS

Self-Aware AI
D-12

Strategic AI
D-11

Tactical AI
D-10

Deep
Learning
D-09

D-01
Sensor
Capture

D-02
Sensor
Fusion

D-03
Virtual
World
Model

D-04
System
Action
Plan

D-05
Controls
Activation

Devices
○ Mono camera
○ Stereo camera
○ LiDAR
○ Radar
○ Ultrasonic
○ GPS
○ IMU
○ Engine
○ Audio
○ Occupants
○ Mobile
○ Controls
○ Etc.

Automobile & CAN   D-06
In-Car Commands   D-07
V2X Communication   D-08

Economic   D-13
Societal   D-14
Innovation D-15

Lance B. Eliot

CHAPTER 2

RESPONSIBILITY AND SELF-DRIVING CARS

Lance B. Eliot

CHAPTER 2

RESPONSIBILITY AND SELF-DRIVING CARS

How do you get people to behave responsibly? That's a refrain right now being asked and pondered regarding the scooter wars underway in cities such as San Francisco and Santa Monica.

In case you've not yet been indoctrinated into the scooter wars, allow me a moment to bring you into the fold.

Companies are springing up like wildflowers that are providing motorized scooter rentals and are using a modern-day approach to do so. Rather than the prospective customer having to go to a storefront to rent a scooter, they instead look for one on a mobile app that shows a GPS map with scooter locations, akin to the Uber mobile app that shows ridesharing car locations, and simply go over to the nearest scooter, rent it with a credit card, it unlocks, and you are good to go. There is an electronic lock on the scooter and whomever last rented it is pretty much allowed to leave it wherever they want to do so (it locks after the renter is done with the scooter). No need to take the scooter back to the rental office. No need to pick it up from a rental office.

Imagine that you are somewhere in Santa Monica and you want to get across town. You could potentially walk it, but that's old fashioned, it might take a long time, and you'd likely not have much fun along the way. You could use a ridesharing service, but why do so when it's a nice day out and the distance is just a mile or two, plus the cost might

31

be relatively high for such a short distance. It would be nifty if somehow there was a motorized scooter, in good shape, waiting for you, and close to where you are now standing. Voila, just use the modern-day scooter rental. Bird is probably the most well-known such scooter rental right now and it seems to be the darling of the venture capital crowd.

It all seems like a win-win. Good for the customer, good for the rental firm. But I've mentioned earlier here that there is a scooter war going on. What could be wrong with the scooter rental equation? Answer, people are doing things they should not be doing. Human behavior, it's a thing.

First, the human "driving" the scooter is supposed to obey the rules of the road. You must not ride on sidewalks (unless there are allowed exceptions, which are few). You can't run red lights. You must stop at stop signs. You must obey the usual traffic laws. Guess what, many of the scooter renters are not abiding by the traffic laws. Shocking? Not really.

Second, there are often local helmet laws that require the use of a helmet when riding a motorized scooter. Bird will actually provide you with a free helmet if you sign-up with them (they mail you the helmet). Guess what, many of the scooter renters are not wearing helmets. Shocking? Not really.

Third, scooter "drivers" have been commonly seen cutting off cars, cutting off bicyclists, cutting off pedestrians. They have been known to zip through crowds at outdoor malls and also try to weave in and out of sidewalks teaming with people. Dangerous for all. Completely wrong to do. Shocking? Not really.

These scooters can typically go around 15 miles per hour, which is plenty fast when using it near people and onto sidewalks and other areas containing pedestrians. There has been an uptick in injuries for scooter riders, including cuts, abrasions, and head injuries. For the mere price of about one dollar to unlock the scooter, and then at a cost of about 15 cents per minute, you can have the joy and adventure of your life. You get to work faster. You think you are a race car driver.

Meanwhile, those that abuse the scooter capability are apt to make life difficult and dangerous for everyone else.

There are even concerns about where the scooters are being placed while not in use. Some renters just put the scooter wherever they darned well please. Sometimes they place it in front of a store, blocking the entrance and exit of the store. Sometimes they place it in a driveway, blocking vehicles from readily going into and out of the driveway. It's like discarding trash and not having to worry about putting the trash into a proper receptacle. You reach your desired destination, step off the scooter, indicate you are done renting it via your mobile app, and walk away from the scooter. Why should you care that it now possibly is in the way of others? Shocking? Not really.

The scooter rental firms like Bird have tended to defend their business model by indicating that they do all sorts of things to prevent people from misusing the scooters. When you sign-up for the scooter rental, it tells you to not do the things I've just mentioned that people are doing in droves. On the screen, it tells you to obey the traffic laws. It tells you to not use the scooter in ways that can endanger people. It tells you that you need to wear a helmet if the local laws say you do (and some, like Bird, can provide you one, though you need to remember to take it with you). Blah, blah, blah.

Why did I say blah, blah, blah? Because there are now opponents of these scooter rentals that say that it is insufficient to simply notify people that they need to obey the law, and that they need to wear helmets, and so on. It has little teeth. It is an attempt of these firms to provide a product or service that in the end is dangerous, and yet they can pretend that they have warned the renter "drivers" of what they need to do and not do. Not enough, say the opponents. These scooter rental firms are raking in the dough and trying to act like they are innocent and that it is solely up the renter "driver" to take responsibility for their own actions.

What does this have to do with AI self-driving cars, you might be wondering?

At the Cybernetic AI Self-Driving Car Institute, we are asking the same kinds of questions about AI self-driving cars, and trying to find ways to deal with the similar problems being encountered.

Of course, it's a bit more serious in the sense that if you have human drivers that do not abide by certain kinds of necessary practices with a self-driving car, the end result can be real life-or-death consequences. A mishandled car is a much more dangerous machine and potential killer than is a scooter.

The Case of Tesla's Marketing and Advertising

Recently, a letter was submitted to the Federal Trade Commission by a consumer watchdog group that asserts that Tesla is doing essentially what I've described about the scooter rentals. Tesla is accused of deceptive and misleading statements and actions, all of which are contributing to Tesla drivers potentially becoming endangered, and now there are some actual cases involving Tesla related driving deaths that are claimed to support this notion.

It has been pointed out that the web site touting the Tesla Autopilot indicates that the Tesla car says this rather prominently "Full Self-Driving Hardware on All Cars," and that there is video that begins with this emboldened message shown on the screen (shown in all caps on the video): "THE PERSON IN THE DRIVER'S SEAT IS ONLY THERE FOR LEGAL REASONS. HE IS NOT DOING ANYTHING. THE CAR IS DRIVING ITSELF."

What impression do you get from those aspects?

Do you believe that the self-driving car can drive the car without human intervention? For those of you that are AI developers and know about AI self-driving cars, you'd for sure be saying that of course you know that the Autopilot doesn't truly drive the car without any human intervention. But, what about the average consumer? What impression would they get?

It is contended that most people would think that the Tesla Autopilot is a true Level 5 self-driving car, which is the level at which an AI self-driving car is driven by the AI and there is no human assistance needed. Indeed, many auto makers and tech firms that are aiming toward Level 5 self-driving cars are making them so that there aren't any driver controls in them at all, at least none for humans to use. The notion is that the AI is the driver of the car. There is no human driving.

Tesla's Autopilot is currently considered somewhere around a Level 2 or Level 3. It absolutely requires that a human driver be present, and that the human driver be ready to take over control of the car. It is not in that sense a true self-driving car (i.e., it is not a Level 5). And yet, some would say that the manner in which Tesla is marketing and promoting the car would tend to mislead consumers into believing that it is a true self-driving car.

Another common complaint about Tesla's approach is that they have "cleverly" named their AI system to be called Autopilot. What impression do you have of the word "autopilot" in general?

For most people, they tend to think of an airplane autopilot, of which, they assume that it means that an airplane can be flown without the need for a human pilot to intervene. We've all seen TV shows and movies wherein the human pilot turns on the autopilot, and then reads the newspaper or maybe even falls asleep. That's the general notion that people seem to have about the word autopilot. Does then the naming of the Tesla Autopilot also contribute to deceiving people into believing that the AI of the Tesla at this stage of capability is more capable than it really is?

Meanwhile, the deadly Tesla driving incidents of May 2016 and March 2018 have been assessed so far as occurring as a result of the human driver failing to do their part in terms of driving the car, and for which it is then been stated by the NTSB in the May 2016 case that the human driver had a "pattern of use of the Autopilot system indicated an over-reliance on the automation and a lack of understanding of the system limitations."

Furthermore, each time that there has been a Tesla incident involving an activated Autopilot, the Tesla company has right away pointed the finger at the human driver. The human driver was not paying attention, they say. The use of the Autopilot requires an active human driver, they say, and emphasize that the Tesla owner's manual states this, along with an on-screen message. According to the NHTSA though, "it's not enough to put it in an owners' manual and hope that drivers will read it and follow it."

Tesla claims that the human drivers do know that they are key to the driving task, as based on surveys that Tesla has conducted. Thus, when an accident occurs such as the March 2018 incident, they pointed out that: "The driver had received several visual and one audible hands-on warning earlier in the drive and the driver's hands were not detected on the wheel for six seconds prior to the collision." In other words, it is being implied that the human driver should have known — and was in a sense warned to be in-the-know, and yet the human driver failed to do so, and thus presumably the human driver is then responsible for the incident and not the auto maker.

Some accuse Tesla of wanting to have their cake and eat it too, in that on the one hand it wants to promote its Autopilot as the greatest thing since sliced bread, and yet at the same time try to retreat from any such implication when it comes time to own up when an accident occurs. There are some that suggest it is like in the movie Casablanca, wherein the French Captain Louis Renault pretends to look the other way and tells the police to round-up the usual suspects, when he really knows who done it.

Tesla points out that they intentionally have the steering wheel touch sensor in order to act as a continual reminder to the human driver to remain attentive to the driving task. Some experts have said they should have done more, such as using eye movement detection and face monitoring to be able to be assured that the driver is actually watching the road ahead. It was recently revealed in an account in the Wall Street Journal that Tesla had considered adding such equipment but decided not to do so, which may come back to bite them.

Will the Federal Trade Commission opt to investigate the claim against Tesla of having deceptive and misleading advertising and marketing practices?

No one knows.

If they do open an investigation, it would certainly seem to cast a shadow over Tesla and its Autopilot. Tesla already seems to be facing a number of other issues and this might be another weight on the camel's back. Or, it could be seen as something minor and more of the usual kind of bravado that many of the tech firms seem to exhibit. Also, there are some that feel any regulation that looks over the shoulder of self-driving car makers is going to stunt the growth and pace of advance for AI self-driving cars, and so there is resistance toward taking action against these makers.

Even if an official investigation is launched, it could be that Tesla might try to settle the matter rather than having to duke it out and have the public become concerned or confused as to what the fuss is all about. Some suggest that Tesla could readily change the name of the Autopilot and try to re-brand it, selecting a name that would perhaps have less of a connotation baggage associated with it. They could also increase the manner in which they warn human drivers about the capabilities of the car. All of this could be done to appease the regulator and yet not cause a dent particularly in the allure of Tesla.

I've already warned that for all of the AI self-driving car makers and tech firms, we're are gradually and inexorably moving toward an era of product liability lawsuits.

I've also warned about how the auto makers and tech firms are going to market AI self-driving cars, and that it can provide both an impetus for the public to want and accept AI self-driving cars, but it could also backfire if the expectations are not met.

One way to consider this problem involves an equation with some aspects to the left of the equal sign, and other aspects to the right of the equal sign. On the left, we'll stack the suggested and overt claims made by an auto maker or tech firm about what the AI self-driving car can do. On the right, we'll stack what the AI self-driving car can actually do. Right now, some would say that Tesla has too much on the left, and so the equation is unbalanced in comparison to what is on the right side of the equation.

Presumably, any such auto maker or tech firm needs to reach a balanced equation, and to do so will either need to subtract something from the left to bring it down to the actual capabilities indicated on the right side of the equation, or, they will need to increase the capabilities on the right side to match the inflated expectations on the left side. By far, changing the left side is faster to achieve than changing the right side.

Responsibility and AI Self-Driving Cars

Let's revisit the scooter wars. Who is responsible for the proper use of the motorized scooters that are being rented? You might say that it is the human "driver" that has rented the scooter, they are the responsible party. This seems to make sense. They rented it, they should use it properly. There are those though that say the scooter rental firm is responsible, they are the responsible party. This seems to make sense. They provided the scooter for rental, and so they should be ensuring that however it is used that it is used in a proper manner.

This can be likened to AI self-driving cars.

Who is responsible for an AI self-driving car and its actions?

You might say that the human driver is the responsible party. Or, you might say that the auto maker is the responsible party. We might also consider that it could be the AI system that's responsible, or maybe the AI maker, or perhaps an insurance firm that is insuring the self-driving car, or maybe the human occupants (even if not driving the vehicle).

Take a look at Figure 1.

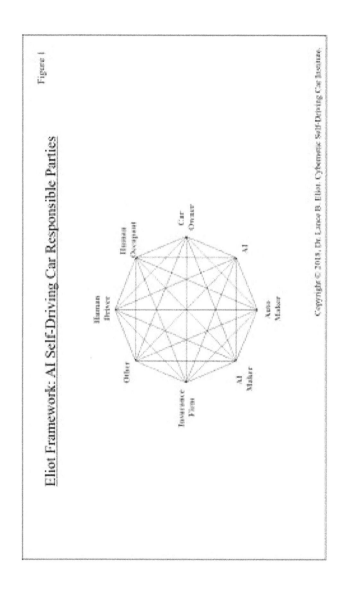

Is it only one of those parties that holds the sole and entire responsibility?

Maybe. You might contend it is solely and completely the human driver that is to be held responsible for the action of the AI self-driving car. Or, maybe you take the position that it is solely and completely the auto maker. The odds are that we'll likely consider it to be some kind of shared responsibility. It might be a combination of the auto maker and the AI makers that are held responsible. Or, maybe a combination of the auto maker, the AI maker, and the human driver.

See Figure 2.

In the case of the AI self-driving car, we need to consider the level of the self-driving car.

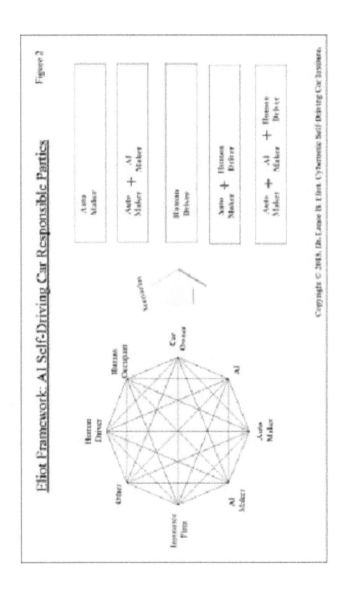

At the Level 5, the true self-driving car, we presumably can say that it is not the responsibility of the human driver since presumably there will not be a human driver and not even a provision to have a human driver in the self-driving car (all humans will be mere occupants, not drivers).

See Figure 3.

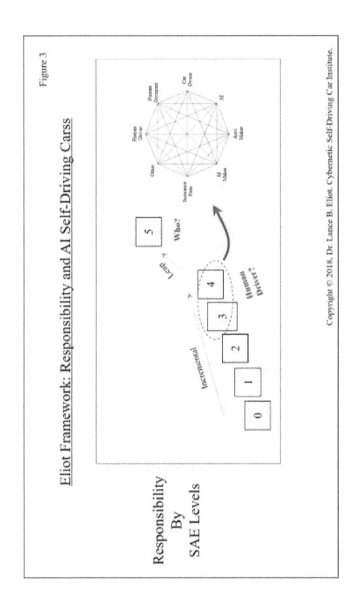

Figure 3

When we're in the levels less than 5, it's pretty much the standard definition that the human driver is responsible for the actions of the self-driving car. But, there's definite wiggle room since the AI could have done something untoward, and thus it raises the question of whether even a human driver that was attentive and ready to take action, whether or not the human can still be held responsible.

I've analyzed this in my exploration of the human back-up drivers that are currently being used in self-driving cars that are being tested on our public roadways. Suppose you put a human driver into a self-driving car, you tell them they are ultimately responsible for the actions of the car, but then when an accident is about to happen the AI hands-over the car controls to the human with only a split-second left to go. Can the human be reasonably expected to really take any action? Is it "fair and reasonable" to still say that it was the human driver at fault?

Co-Shared Responsibility

When I was in college, I moved into a house with three other roommates, having come from my own apartment that had just me in it. I at first thought it would be a blast and we'd have nonstop fun, kind of our own version of Animal House. What I discovered pretty quickly was that the food I left in the refrigerator would mysteriously disappear (this never happened in my own apartment!). We had one bathroom for all of us, and invariably it was turned into a pig sty, and nobody took responsibility for how it got that way (just by osmosis, I guess).

Things got so bad that we had a toilet paper roll "battle" that consisted of no one wanting to go to the trouble to put a new toilet roll into the bathroom (it would have meant having the foresight to buy a roll and have it ready, and actually take the old one off and put the new one on). As the toilet paper roll neared the end of its available tissues, we all began taking less and less, in hopes that someone else would get stuck with the roll being essentially empty and then forced into changing the paper roll. We'd end-up with one ply left. Then, one half of that (a household member used just half for the needed purpose). Then, half of that half (it's amazing and surprising how much a quarter of a ply can do for you). And so on. It's funny to think about it now, but we were actually serious about it at the time.

The point to the story is that when in a shared responsibility situation, you need to have some pretty clear-cut rules about how the responsibility is to be shared. If you don't have ground rules, it can be chaos, since the joint responsibility is muddled.

Take a look at Figure 4.

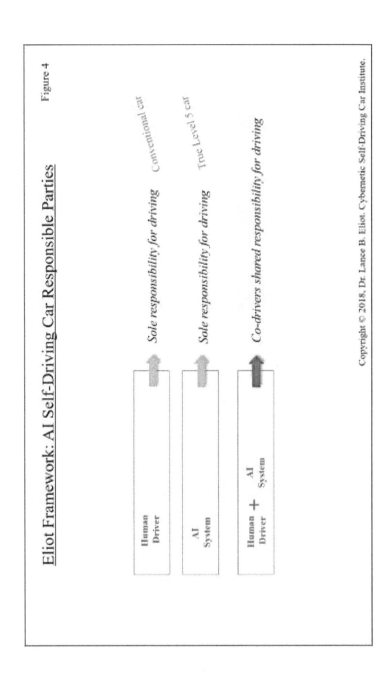

Eliot Framework: AI Self-Driving Car Responsible Parties

Figure 4

Human Driver — *Sole responsibility for driving* — Conventional car

AI System — *Sole responsibility for driving* — True Level 5 car

Human Driver + AI System — *Co-drivers shared responsibility for driving*

For a conventional car, I think we can pretty much agree that the human driver is the responsible party. Of course, there are exceptions, such as if the wheels fall off the car because the auto maker made them defective, etc.

With less-than-Level 5 self-driving car, we're going to have a co-shared responsibility. Now, I'm not necessarily talking about legal responsibility for the moment and would like to just take a look at the more practical technical aspects about this co-sharing arrangement.

Here's where the rub is. When you put the AI system and the human driver into a co-shared responsibility situation, they each need to "know" what the other is supposed to do. This also needs to be achieved in some practical manner. I say this because many of the AI developers and the auto makers and tech firms are not treating this in a truly practical way.

Let's consider some of the key ways in which the responsibility can get muddled and focus on the human driver aspects thereof: (See Fig. 5.)

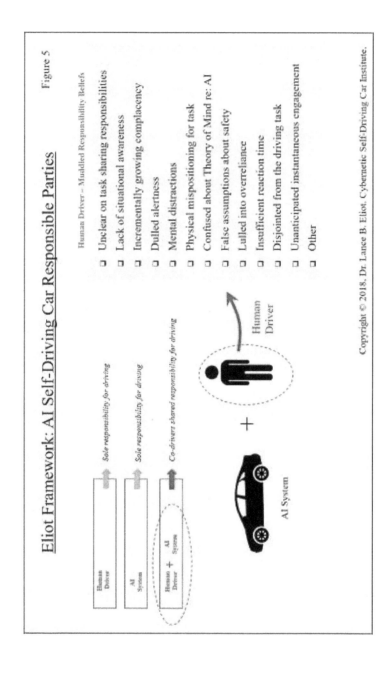

Figure 5

- Unclear on task sharing responsibilities

First of all, the human driver needs to be completely and utterly clear about the task sharing duties. Who does what, and when, and why, and how. This is not easy to ensure. Humans, as we've seen with the scooters, will tend to ignore warnings and cautions, and do what they think they want to do. Same goes for AI self-driving cars.

- Lack of situational awareness

The human driver tends to drift away from the situational awareness that normally occurs when they are fully responsible for the driving task. It is easy to begin to believe that the situation is being handled, and so you don't need to stay on the edge of your seat. The problem is that when the human driver is needed, it often involves a split-second decision and action, all of which depend on having an immediate situational awareness.

- Incrementally growing complacency

Humans tend to get complacent. If the AI seems to be driving, and the more that it happens, the more complacent you become. You aren't thinking about those instantaneous situations like a tire blowing out or a truck that is mistakenly parked in the middle of the road. Most of our daily driving is relatively routine. The AI generally handles routine driving. Therefore, humans become complacent.

- Dulled alertness

Humans alertness gets dulled. You really can't expect someone to be watching out continuously when they are under the belief that the AI is generally able to drive the car. When you are solely driving the car, you know that you need to be alert. When "someone else" (something else) is driving the car, you let your guard down.

- Mental distractions

When you are solely driving a car, you might have some mental distractions like you are thinking about what you are going to wear to that party tonight. But, you still have at the forefront the driving task. When you have the AI doing the driving, you tend to allow mental distractions to takeover more of your mental processing. It's a natural tendency.

- Physical mispositioning for task

Most of the time, if you are solely driving a car, you have your foot on the gas or the brake, you have your hands on the wheel, all of this is continuous. When you are sharing the driving with the AI, you are likely to take your feet off the peddles, and your hands off the wheel. Even if you are timed and need to periodically put your hands on the wheel, this is not the same as continuously having your hands on the wheel.

- Confused about Theory of Mind re: AI

This is one aspect that not many are considering, namely, the human driver needs to have a theory of mind about the AI driving capability. This is akin to if I had a novice teenage driver at the wheel of my car. I would generally know what the teenage driver can handle and not handle. Right now, few of the human drivers have a sufficient understanding of the theory of mind about what the AI can and cannot do.

- False assumptions about safety

The human driver tends to believe that if an accident hasn't yet happened while the AI is driving, it probably implies there won't be an accident. The longer that the AI drives and seems to be accident free, the more this false assumption about safety increases.

- Lulled into overreliance

The human driver begins to become over reliant on the AI driving the car. You've likely seen the videos of those idiots that put their head out the window of the car and speak to the video camera about how great it is that the AI is driving the car. All it would take is for that car to get into a predicament and that head-out-the-window driver would likely get injured or killed (or, lose their head).

- Insufficient reaction time

This is one of the most insidious aspects about a co-shared responsibility. Imagine a teenage driver that was about to ram into a brick wall and suddenly looked at you, the adult sitting in the passenger seat, and told you to take the wheel. Too little, too late. This is what is going to keep happening with today's AI self-driving cars.

- Disjointed from the driving task

Inevitably, the human driver is going to feel disjointed from the driving task. Even if you put all sorts of facial monitoring and eye monitoring, it's an instinctive kind of aspect that you are no longer solely responsible and so you feel less committed to the driving task. This is human nature.

- Unanticipated instantaneous engagement

This idea that the human driver will need to become instantaneously engaged in the driving task, when meanwhile they've been only partially engaged, and that it will most likely occur in an unanticipated moment, this is another one of those seemingly impractical notions.

- Other

You might already be aware that Google's Waymo has been keen to develop an AI self-driving car and has tended towards achieving a Level 5. Why? One reason likely is that it removes the co-sharing of the driving task. This eliminates all of the above human frailties and issues of design and development related to getting the human and the automation to work together in a coordinated and blissful manner.

There's also the aspect that having AI that can fully drive a car without human intervention is a much more challenging technical aspect, since you presumably need to make the AI so good that it can drive like humans can. When you have a self-driving car that has a co-shared responsibility, you can always lean on the human to make up the slack for whatever you could not get the AI to be able to do. Some see this as a half-baked technical solution.

For those auto makers and tech firms in the middle ground, above the low-tech conventional car and not yet at the true Level 5, it's going to be ugly times for all.

Those that naively think that they can just push technology out the door and expect humans to play along, well, perhaps the scooter wars are a good lesson. You can make seemingly wonderful technology, but those darned humans are not going to abide by what you want them to do. Is this then an excuse for you? I don't think so. I assert that making a better mousetrap means more than just the technology itself, and that you have to take into account the nature of humans, else in the end it's going to be a deathtrap. AI self-driving cars are a serious innovation and I hope it's not going to get undermined, perhaps inadvertently in the rush to get it onto our streets and yet in the end produce untoward results that will kill the golden goose for all of us, society included.

CHAPTER 3

CHANGING LANES
AND
SELF-DRIVING CARS

CHAPTER 3

CHANGING LANES
AND SELF-DRIVING CARS

Hey buddy, pick a lane and stick with it. I can't believe that driver just cut into my lane. I need to quickly move into the lane next to me. There's a car blocking my lane up ahead. There aren't enough lanes here for the number of cars. These lanes are poorly marked and cars are veering toward each other. Which lane am I supposed to be in. The emergency lane is nowhere to be seen. Drivers are illegally going into and out of the HOV lane.

You've likely thought about or spoken aloud those preceding remarks about roadway lanes. We live in a world of lanes. On the open highways, maybe there are a couple of lanes going in each direction. On some freeways, there are at times five lanes going in each direction. On a mountain road, you usually have one lane in each direction, and on occasion it narrows to just one lane with the need to be extra cautious for any cars coming in the opposite direction.

Lanes can be marked in a variety of ways. Sometimes there are bots dots that when you go across them it causes your tires and car to rumble, warning you that you just crossed a lane. There are some lanes that are marked with flat paint, and so there's no "feeling" about crossing a lane and it's all based on visual sight. There might not be any markings at all, and it's just a gut feel as to where the lanes are supposed to be. In addition, there can be special occasions when a lane is marked by orange cones, creating a temporary lane such as after a car crash and the police are trying to redirect traffic.

Until the day arrives that we have flying cars, we all need to be cognizant of roadway lanes. It's kind of amazing when you think about it that people are all willing to most of the time obey the lanes. Each morning, during my lengthy commute on the freeway, I watch and marvel that the drivers generally agree to stay in their lanes. They don't have to per se. You could straddle two lanes, and there's nothing immediate that would stop you from doing so. There isn't a freeway laser that would zap your car, and no big hammer that would bang on your car to get it to move over. Nope, we just all voluntarily abide by the lanes.

We do so partially because of the law. As a driver, you don't want to get a ticket and so you obey the lanes. Also, you pretty much know that there will be fellow-driver vigilante justice extracted if you are straddling lanes excessively. Other cars will honk at you, and at times maybe aim at you to force you in a chicken-game like way to get into a lane. I'm not suggesting that drivers aren't straddling lanes from time-to-time, and likewise they often make really bad decisions about lane changes, but I am just saying that most of the time it's kind of a miracle that all these people driving all these multi-ton deadly machines -- and for which at any moment they could do whatever they want, we don't have utter chaos. We're pretty much all well behaved most of the time.

Thanks goes to all you drivers for a general consensus on sanity when driving.

For teenage drivers that are learning to drive, they often find that changing lanes is one of the scariest aspects of driving a car. Should I go now, or should I wait? Can I make the lane change or will I cut-off another car? Is that car going to allow me into that lane? Should I speed-up? Should I slow down? I remember when I was first learning to drive a car, and we had five high school students in my driver ed class, and for which (scarily) we always all drove in one car with the driving instructor. Each student would get about ten minutes of driving time per instructional trip.

One of the students would make a lane change that took maybe four minutes long and did an inch at a time to get into another lane. It was agonizingly slow. Dangerously slow. In contrast, we had one student driver that made a lane change the instant the instructor said to do so, and at times we nearly got into a car crash because of the rapid movement (it was as though the car dove into the other lane). The moment the instructor started to utter the words "start to think about a lane change," the student took this to mean "get over into the next lane, darn it, as fast as possible, and don't delay since we'll all die if you do." We all held are breaths every time that student got behind the wheel.

Of course, changing lanes is a dangerous act. Think about what can go wrong. You can start the lane change, and perhaps not realize there is a car directly abreast of you, and then hit that car. Or, maybe that car realizes you are mistakenly getting into their lane and so they hit you, or they veer and hit another car as "caused" by your having started your lane change. Let's assume you are good enough that you don't start the lane change when there's a car next to you, but once you engage in the move a car "suddenly" appears in that lane. Once again, the chances of getting hit, or hitting the other car, or starting a cascading accident that will possibly injure or even kill other people is all heightened.

There are some key factors involved in the lane change act. One of those factors is speed. Making lane changes at a low speed is more likely to have less adverse consequences. If you hit another car and you are both going 5 miles per hour, it's not a good thing, but hitting another car while going 70 miles per hour is certainly apt to have more dire consequences. The faster speeds tend to mean less reaction time, and so less chance of avoiding a collision. The faster speeds tend to mean greater damage to the cars and greater chances of injury to the human occupants. Faster speeds tend to mean that the incident will turn into a domino and lead to a multitude of crashes.

Believe it or not, I know one driver that genuinely believes that higher speeds are better (safer) for making lane changes. His logic is that the length of time involved in actually undertaking the lane change is reduced. At 70 miles per hour, he says it is a blink of the eye when you make a lane change. It's like being the Flash and it happens so quickly that essentially nothing can go wrong. At slower speeds, he believes it is worse since you take too long to make a lane change. This longer time frame increases the opportunity for a car collision. All I can say is, wow, what a way of thinking. I'm just glad that he and I are rarely on the roadways at the same time.

This does bring up the useful facet that we have both your speed as a factor and also time as a factor. You need to know what your speed is, assuming you want to make a reasonably well executed lane change. You need to know how much time it will take to make your lane change. You need to estimate how much time there will be for a gap to exist in the other lane, such that you can get into that gap. You need to calculate whether you need to speed-up or slow down to make it into that gap. The gap is both a physical gap in terms of physical space where your car can fit and that no other car occupies, and it is a time gap in that it needs to happen at a point in time during which there isn't another car there.

It's physics!

You might be tempted to think that changing lanes is merely a series of algorithmic like calculations that we humans are making. I would suggest that's over simplifying the beauty, art, and craft of lane changing.

You need to be part psychologist too. Will that other driver in the lane next to me be willing to let me in? There's a momentary gap in space and time right now, but in the next few seconds it could disappear. The other car might suddenly accelerate and end-up in the spot that I think I want to occupy. Your lane change is actually a forecast about the future. You are trying to predict what the roadway situation will be in a few seconds from now. This involves making educated guesses. You can't usually know for a certainty what the future is going to hold.

Yes, there are situations involving easy lane change actions. If I'm on the open highway, and there's not any cars around me for miles, I can change lanes to my heart's content. When I was first learning to drive, me and one of my best buddies would sometimes take long drives just to get better at driving, and we'd do a series of lane changes over and over. We'd be on the open highway, and make a lane change. No reason to do so per se. Then make another lane change, and another, and so on. It was for the sake of practice. Anyone watching the car would have thought we were drunk or crazy, since there didn't seem to be any rhyme or reason for the multitude of lane changes.

For ease of discussing lane changes, let's refer to the driver that is initiating the lane change as the activator. The car that is in the other lane that might be impacted by the activator will be referred to as the responder. I'll take the core elements first, namely assume we have one activator and one responder. That being said, this can readily become more complex by adding multiple responders. Or, we could have multiple activators (several cars all wanting to make lane changes at the same time and place). The most reduced and simplest instance would be one activator and zero responders (that's akin to my example above about me and my buddy making lane changes when no other cars were anywhere near us).

Consider first the speeds involved.

I'll use this notation: **Activator: Responder**.

We'll also keep things simple by pretending that the speeds are either high or low.

We then have this:
- High: High
- Low: Low
- High: Low
- Low: High

In the first case, both the activator car and the responder car are going at a high speed. We'll assume for simplicity they are going at the same speed. Generally, the time to make the lane change will be compressed because of the high speeds. Generally, the risk factor will be higher (in spite of what my friend believes about this!) since they are both going at a high speed.

In the second case, both the activator car and the responder car are going at a low speed. We'll assume for simplicity they are going at the same speed. Generally, the time to make the lane change will be longer than the high speeds instance. Generally, the risk factor is lower.

In next two cases, there is a disparity between the speeds of the two cars. This generally creates a situation less clear cut than when both cars are at the same speeds. In the instance of the activator going at a high speed and merging into a lane with a responder at a lower speed, presumably the activator has some advantage since they can readily get ahead of the responder and potentially avoid having the responder strike them from the rear. In comparison, when the activator is going at a low speed and tries to merge in front of a car that is at a high speed, this can be of quite heightened risk since the responder car is going to have to likely react.

This brings up another factor, namely the ability to accelerate and decelerate (brake). We all know that when making a lane change you don't necessarily maintain your existing speed. You can, but often you speed-up to make the lane change, or you slow down. Likewise, the responder might speed-up or slow down.

We now return to the psychology of the lane change act. The activator does not particularly know how the responder will react to the lane change. It could be that the responder might suddenly speed-up, and thus the prediction about the future physical/time gap is no longer what was predicted. Sometimes a responder doesn't want to let the other car into their lane. Sometimes the responder is oblivious to the lane change and just decided to speed-up due to a completely unrelated aspect.

How does another driver know that you are trying to undertake a lane change? Legally, you are supposed to signal that you want to make a lane change. Much of the time, people do indeed turn on their signal blinker. This though can be slippery. Some lane changers will turn on their signal after they've already intruded into the other lane. This could be because they forgot to use the signal and then suddenly remembered, or it could be that they didn't want to give a heads-up beforehand and then as a pretend afterward turned on the signal to act as though they had properly signaled to make a lane change.

In that sense, lane changes involve head-fakes. A head-fake in this context is when you begin to move your car toward a lane change, and though you haven't made a full commitment to it, you are "signaling" that you are making a lane change (this can occur either while using the turn signal or not using the turn signal). So, we have the potential of a head-fake to showcase an upcoming lane change, and we have the use of an actual turn signal.

We have these combinations:
- Head-fake (no): Turn signal (yes)
- Head-fake (no): Turn signal (no)
- Head-fake (yes): Turn signal (yes)
- Head-fake (yes): Turn signal (no)

An activator might not do a head-fake and do just the turn signal. Here, though, there are times that the activator turns on the turn signal but then chooses to not make the lane change. Or, they turn on the turn signal, leave it on, and don't realize they are telegraphing to the rest of the traffic that a lane change is coming. This can be irritating to other drivers, since they are all waiting to witness the lane change and it doesn't arise. I'm sure you've seen drivers that leave on their turn signal and drive mindlessly with it on – you ask yourself, how can they not know their turn signal is on, are they not watching the road and paying attention to their own car?

There's the instance of the no head-fake and no turn signal, and yet the driver makes the lane change anyway. No notice. No trying to be civil. They just suddenly and at times inexplicably make a lane change. This unexpected move can be especially dangerous since none of the nearby drivers have been forwarded about the movement.

There's the use of both the head-fake and the turn signal, which often is handy since it reinforces each other as a means to suggest that the person is really truly going to make a lane change. And then there's the head-fake but no turn signal indication. In this case, the head-fake is considered a stronger suggestion that a lane change is coming, more so than the turn signal. It would be nice though to also have the turn signal as a reinforce that the person is not just maybe weaving and not actually intending to make a lane change.

What does all of this have to do with AI self-driving cars?

At the Cybernetic AI Self-Driving Car Institute, we are developing AI software for self-driving cars and one of the areas that is rapidly being advanced involves lane changes.

For most of the self-driving cars of today, if you ever watch them make a lane change, you might laugh at what you see. Generally, they make a lane change like a timid teenage novice driver would do. The AI of today will only make the lane change if it seems absolutely abundantly the case that the lane change can be made with a great deal of safety.

As such, the AI often starts toward doing a lane change a lot sooner than most human drivers would. Also, the AI self-driving car tends to often disrupt traffic flow when making a lane change, which is not by design but by the aspect that imagine if you had a teenage driver making a lane change on a busy freeway. The other drivers would all pretty quickly size up that driver and either give them wide berth, or try to take advantage of them. This is like playing a game of poker and a rube sits down to play. Everyone else that knows how to play poker will try every trick under the sun on that rube.

I realize that some of you are going to say that there's no need for an AI self-driving car to worry about driving around humans because we are going to have all cars on the road become AI self-driving cars. Wake-up! It's going to be a long, long, long time before that happens. There are about 200 million conventional cars in the United States alone. We are going to have self-driving cars mixing with human driven cars for a very long time.

Recall that I mentioned that making lane changes is not just the act of making calculations. It is also involves the psychology of the other drivers. For human drivers, right now they can easily guess the "psychology" of the AI self-driving cars – just assume that the AI will pretty much do whatever is the most conservative and novice act of changing lanes, and that's it. Having to figure out other humans is more complex, though seasoned drivers have already assessed how to do so. Seasoned drivers look at not only the behavior exhibited by the car and the car driver, but also often include looking to see what the driver looks like, what the car looks like, whether the car is in good shape or bad shape, etc.

The AI of today's AI self-driving cars doesn't consider any of those other aspects. Instead, the AI simplistically detects that there's another object that is moving at such-and-such speed, and otherwise doesn't really care as to the nature of the car, nor the nature of the driver of that car, or any other such facets. It's all calculations based.

Some interesting new approaches to the mathematics of this include incorporating what are called buffer zones. Imagine that the AI self-driving car has a cone around it, which is a buffer zone. Other cars have likewise buzzer zones around them. This virtual buffer zone is a "pretend" in that we are pretending that the car is actually larger than it is. You might think of this as a geo-fence placed around the car. The buffer zone can be wide, like say we decide that there's a pretend area around a car that's 4 feet wide, all around the car. Or, the buffer zone might be tight, such as perhaps a foot in size.

When trying to make a lane change, we'll mathematically consider that the objects (the cars) are the sizes of their buffer zones. One key principle is that we don't want to have buffer zones come in contact with each other. If the buffer zones come in contact, it presumably implies a collision is going to occur. Now, the question arises as to how risky we are going to go. If the buffer zone is four feet, I presumably have some allowable slippage that I can make the lane change and get say within three feet of the other car, and not actually hit the other car, even though I've punched into their buffer zone.

Mathematically, we'd like to have the AI be able to "prove" that collision avoidance will be preserved.

So, we take the buffer zone of the activator, and the buffer zone of the responder, we make assumptions about their speeds and likely actions in the near future of when the lane change will happen, and run through the calculations to see whether the lane change can be made with a guarantee of no collision.

This is easy to do in the lab or via a simulator. In the real-world, this needs to be done in real-time. The question arises as to whether or not the calculations can be done quickly enough to then make the decision for the lane change and then do the lane change. If the calculations take say 3 seconds too long, the opportunity for the lane change evaporates. Furthermore, the whole set of calculations now is worthless since the circumstances have changed and a new set needs to be executed.

As much as possible, it is best to pre-compute this. You can have on-board the AI system lots of pre-computations done for varying circumstances, and thus instead of having to calculate at the moment, you look up in tables to see what those tables indicate. This is similar to chess playing. You can either have a chess playing program that has to calculate all the various permutations and options of play, or you can have pre-stored templates that once the chessboard is in a certain configuration, you just look it up and know what the next move should be. We can do somewhat of the same with the AI self-driving car and lane changes.

Not entirely though. And so we are more than likely to have to at times make the raw calculations. And, if so, they need to be done in real-time to match the time constraints of the situation. One recent approach by researchers at MIT involves calculating a logistics function involving the buffer zones and the direction, speed, etc., and then combining with a Laplace-Gauss distribution (the "Bell Curve") to do an on-the-fly estimation of the chances of making the lane change and doing so with collision avoidance.

Efforts to solve this problem need to contend with the severe time constraints and doing the calculation in real-time, along with considering how much information is available and how reliable is that information.

The sensors of the self-driving car are providing data about what is around the self-driving car. You cannot assume that this is perfect information. The sensors might be getting a lot of noise such as the cameras have blurry images due to weather conditions, or maybe the radar is not reflecting well off the other cars. Etc. The sensor fusion might be contending with conflicting and missing information about the surroundings.

Changing lanes appears on the surface to be pretty straightforward. As a human, if you are the activator, you just glance over your shoulder, survey the scene, maybe turn on your turn signal, you steer the car into the other lane, and voila you are done. The responder likewise simply has to notice that your car is providing some indication that you are wanting to make a lane change, perhaps via your turn signal and/or your head-fake movement, and then let you in.

I hope that you realize now that making a lane change is a lot harder than it seems. As usual, it's one of those human learned aspects that after a while seems effortless. To get an AI system to do this, with a car, and in motion, and with all the variabilities in terms of the surrounding traffic and the roadway and the lanes, it's a tough thing to do. For the moment, we've gotten the AI to make baby step lane changes. By continuing to push forward and advance the techniques and software, we aim to make lane changes as "effortless" as humans. This includes that at times the lane changes might be civil in nature, and in other cases more aggressive. Soon enough, you might find yourself saying "hey buddy, you cut me off" and then realize you should say "hey AI, you cut me off!"

CHAPTER 4
PROCRASTINATION
AND
SELF-DRIVING CARS

Lance B. Eliot

CHAPTER 4

PROCRASTINATION

AND

SELF-DRIVING CARS

Procrastination. Procrastinator. As the old joke goes, when someone asks you what the word procrastination means, you are supposed to say "I'll get back to you about that."

I'm sure we've all felt like a procrastinator at one time or another. Often considered a negative aspect of human behavior, some liken procrastination with being lazy, careless, and otherwise less desirable than being prompt and proactive.

We might though be somewhat making a false generalization about procrastination. Does being a procrastinator always have to be bad? It is said that prolific and ingenious inventor and artist Leonardo da Vinci was known for dragging out the works he owed his patrons and often taking nearly forever to get done what he had been obligated to produce. Charles Darwin had acknowledged that he often put off things that he was supposed to do or wanted to do. Few realize that he took years to write his acclaimed "On the Origin of Species" and was at times using his time to instead study barnacles. If these greats had bouts with procrastination, can it really be that bad a thing?

If you find yourself falling into the procrastination trap and don't want to be a procrastinator, you can always call upon Saint Expedite. For those of you have been to New Orleans, or have certain religious interests, you likely know that Saint Expedite is considered the patron for those that want to avert being a procrastinator, and you can ask for his assistance in finding rapid solutions to nagging problems. I suppose too, there are some that say you just need to kick yourself in the you-know-where, but anyway it can be hard to stop the urge to procrastinate however you try to prevent it.

Psychologically, it is theorized that people often procrastinate because they fear the act of doing something that might fail. As such, in order to avoid failure, they postpone it. Presumably, by not trying, you convince yourself that you are better off. You might even use trivial items to help yourself be a procrastinator. Should I go to the dentist, or maybe instead I need to wash my socks and clean the latrine? One might think that dealing with the health of your teeth would be a high priority in comparison to those other tasks. It's amazing how we can allow seemingly low-priority items to aid us in avoiding dealing with meatier issues or topics.

For some people, they are an occasional procrastinator. Perhaps most of the time they get things done on a timely basis. A particular situation might cause them to go into a procrastination mode. A personal example is that the other day my car dashboard lit up with an indicator that my low-beam left headlight bulb was burnt out. I probably should have taken my car right away to have the lamp replaced. Instead, I sheepishly admit that for several weeks I drove at night with the high-beams on, rather than the low beams, so that I'd have both headlamps working. I truly meant to go over to have the headlight replaced, but seemed to let other matters take higher priority.

Sometimes a procrastination can have potentially dangerous consequences. You could say that my example about driving around with my high-beams on, rather than using my low beams, made my driving circumstances a bit less safe. Not much less, I'd argue, but certainly a little bit. On the other hand, shortly after I had the left headlight replaced, a few days later my left rear brake light suddenly went out. It was a Murphy's Law kind of curse because had it gone out just a few days earlier, I could have had it replaced at the same time as the headlight. But, no, it had to wait and then force me to make a second trip to the car repair shop. In theory, I could have driven for many days or weeks with the left rear brake light out, but this for sure would have reduced the safety factor of my driving.

There are the perennial or serial procrastinators. These are the types that just seem to shove everything off into the future. No reason to get something done today, if you can hand it off to the future, they believe. They might overtly have this belief and relish it. Others find themselves gradually getting immersed into this approach, happening almost without them consciously realizing they are doing so. It can be a deathly kind of spiral. You beat yourself up for having procrastinated. It happens again. You beat yourself up again. You then become convinced that you are a "failure" and destined to procrastinate. Nothing is going to get you out of that spiral, other than some kind of direct intervention.

There's a well-known theory that somewhat covers this, called Temporal Motivation Theory (TMT). You might find of interest a core formula often used to express TMT:

Motivation = (Expectancy x Value) / (1 + Impulsiveness x Delay)

Your "Motivation" is the amount of desire that you have to achieve a particular outcome. If your motivation score is low, you are more likely to procrastinate. If your motivation score is high, such as if you realize that your brake light being out is putting you in grave danger, you are more likely to take action about it. We can calculate your motivation for a given circumstance.

The "Expectancy" is the probability of achieving success on the matter at hand. The "Value" is the reward that you personally will gain by achieving the desired outcome. By multiplying the Expectancy by the Value, the formula is saying that if one of those variable is low it is going to bring down the combination of them, while if they are both high it will make their combination higher. I think that my expectancy of fixing my brake light is quite high (just need to get the car over to the repair shop), and the value of increasing my safety while driving my car is high.

The "Impulsiveness" is the person's sensitivity to delay. Some people are very impulsive and need to do things right away. Other people are more prone to taking their time or at least considering that they are willing to take time and don't need to immediately handle the matter. There's the "Delay" which is considered the time to realize the needed achievement.

Anyway, it's kind of an interesting formula because it tries to mathematically express something that we all seem to know is happening, but don't have at hand a tangible way to calculate why we do what we do. Using the formula, you can become more reflective when faced with a situation that you are possibly going to procrastinate on. You can ask yourself, why is your motivation so low, and whether it is due to the expectancy, the value, the impulsiveness, or the delay, or possibly some combination of those several factors.

People often make excuses for why they procrastinate. When I refer to these aspects as excuses, I should clarify that maybe they are valid. We often react to the word "excuse" and think it is a made-up aspect or an attempt to deflect blame. Sometimes an excuse is quite valid. It doesn't have to be a cover story or a deflection.

Here's some of the traditional excuses or coping responses:
- Avoidance of the matter
- Denial about the matter
- Trivialization of the matter
- Distraction about the matter
- Mocking of the matter
- Blaming about the matter

This quick introduction to the topic of procrastination then brings us to a major final point before I move onto using this foundation for other purposes herein. I claim that procrastination can occur perchance, but it can also be a manifest strategy.

In the case of my left headlight, I was well aware that I was "procrastinating" about taking in the car to have the headlight replaced. I won't try to convince you that I was so busy that I couldn't take it in (that's a potential "excuse" or coping avoidance). If I had really thought the headlight being out for the low-beam was important, I would have gotten to the car repair promptly. Instead, I made an explicit "procrastination" decision that I would delay taking the car in, and that the use of the high-beam was sufficiently acceptable in the interim.

Someone outside of my situation, looking at what I had done, might label my actions as those of a procrastinator. Okay, if you want to label me that way, for this situation, I'll take it. Is the word "procrastination" in this instance a showing that I am a bad person that is careless and lazy? I don't think so. It merely shows that I had calculated that the delay in doing something was in my view a proper thing to do.

You might wonder if I now have gotten bitten by the procrastination virus and everything I do is infected with procrastination? No, that hasn't happened. Indeed, as mentioned, I opted to right away take care of the brake light, even though it was a hassle as I had just already been the repair shop and so had to go there a second time (wasting my time, in a sense, other than to effect the repair, which could have been presumably done in one visit, had I known the brake light was about to go out too).

What does all of this have to do with AI self-driving cars?

At the Cybernetic AI Self-Driving Car Institute, we are using the core aspects of "procrastination" for two purposes, one is serving as a direct strategy of the AI driving the car, and the other is to deal with what we believe will be a human foible regarding AI self-driving cars.

Let's tackle the human foible topic first.

As I've said many times, an AI self-driving car is still a car. By this I mean that some people are getting into their heads that an AI self-driving car will magically work 24x7 and will never have any mechanical problems or breakdowns. This utopian view of the world assumes that there is some kind of magical fairy dust that we are going to sprinkle onto AI self-driving cars that keeps them from wearing out and from having parts that break. Let's get real. A car is a car. The brake lights are going to go out, just like on a regular car. The oil will need to be changed. The transmission will need to get overhauled.

This is going to actually happen more frequently and with deeper impact since we are expecting AI self-driving cars to be running all the time, versus today the average car is unused nearly most of the day.

Not only will the conventional parts of the self-driving car breakdown, but you can bet that the specialized add-on parts are going to breakdown too. The specialized processors to run the AI systems will eventually start to falter and need to be replaced. The sonar devices will eventually need to be replaced. The radar devices will need to be replaced. And so on.

I hope you now agree that an AI self-driving car is a car. It will have all sorts of mechanical problems over time. This will happen to the conventional parts of the car. This will happen to the specialized parts of the car. We don't hear anything about it today because the few AI self-driving cars on the roadways are living pampered lives. They are like horses that are thoroughbreds. The auto maker or tech firm caters to their every need. These self-driving cars are continually getting primped and revived. The odds of having a part breakdown during one of their journeys is very remote.

Now imagine an AI self-driving car that Joe Smith has purchased and he's using it for himself, for his family, for his friends, and renting it out too for ride sharing. That self-driving car is busy.

When something snaps or breaks on the AI self-driving car, we need to consider these ramifications:

- Does the AI self-driving car realize that something is broken or amiss?

- Can the AI self-driving car continue safely operating?

- Is there anything the AI self-driving car can do to get itself repaired?

We cannot assume that the AI will even know that something on the self-driving car is broken. We're developing our AI self-driving car software to purposely try to detect that something has gone afoul. Many of the auto makers or tech firms consider this to be an "edge" problem. An edge problem is something that you don't consider core to what you are doing. Most of the auto makers and tech firms just want an AI self-driving car to deal with driving the car. Right now, since these self-driving cars are pampered, there's no need to deal with detecting anomalies automatically and having to deal with them immediately and directly.

Here's how procrastination comes to play.

Suppose the human owner becomes aware that some aspect of their AI self-driving car has gone afoul. Maybe an occupant riding in it called the owner to complain. Maybe the AI detected that something was amiss and texted the owner to indicate that the self-driving car is having a problem. What will the human owner do?

You might assume that the human owner will promptly make sure that the AI self-driving car gets repaired. This would happen in the utopian world. In the real-world, we're betting that the human owner is possibly going to procrastinate. If there are say ten cameras on the AI self-driving car, and it's been designed to be able to operate with just nine, though not as good as it could with ten cameras, the human owner might decide to keep the AI self-driving car going and not take it in for repair.

Is this safe? Maybe yes, maybe not. Will the next occupant that gets into that AI self-driving car even know that it is only operating with nine cameras? Possibly not. Should we ensure that the AI of the self-driving car warns any passengers about any anomalies? The owner of the self-driving car might not like that idea, and be worried that as a ride sharing rental that they'll lose money if the AI starts to blab about what is wrong with the self-driving car.

There aren't any regulations that force the AI to reveal what's going on. The owner likewise is not under any direct law to do so, though you could construe various aspects about safety and the public that might turn this into a crime. For the moment, the use of AI for self-driving cars is so new that we have yet to figure out what twists and turns will happen, and nor do we yet know what kinds of regulations and new laws might be required.

The overall point is that we need to anticipate the dangers of potential "procrastination" based on human foibles and how it might adversely impact AI self-driving cars and their safety on our roadways.

Our focus is for the moment aimed at the technical side of things. The AI needs to be able to detect that something is amiss. When this occurs, the AI has to be sophisticated enough to know how to try and overcome the aspect that went afoul, if it can, and be aware of any new limitations that arise (maybe the self-driving car can only go 5 miles per hour and no faster, or maybe it can make right turns but not any left turns, etc.). And, it has to be aware of whom to contact about the matter.

There are some that say this is "easily" solved because once the AI self-driving car detects that something is amiss, it can just route itself to the nearest repair shop. Problem solved.

Well, not quite. Maybe the AI self-driving car is unfit to be able to get to the nearest repair shop. Maybe it is fit to do so, but perhaps it's Okay for it to instead continue on its journey and later on go to the repair shop. Maybe it cannot detect itself that itself is in trouble. As such, the AI should allow for the human occupants to possibly tell it that something is amiss ("we see smoke coming out of the engine compartment"), and possibly even communicate via V2V (vehicle-to-vehicle communications) and be told by another AI self-driving car that something is wrong (self-driving car X12345 transmits a warning to self-driving car Y87654 that there is smoke coming from the engine compartment).

The second part of the procrastination aspect related to AI self-driving cars involves using procrastination as a driving strategy.

I know that you might be somewhat surprised or shocked at this idea of using procrastination purposefully. Remember though that I earlier stated that procrastination can occur by happenstance, or it can be used as a directed strategy.

Suppose I'm driving on the freeway. My exit is up ahead. I do the right thing and long before the exit make my way over to the rightmost lane. I sit there in the slow lane, maybe a mile ahead of my exit. I'm going bumper-to-bumper but it's Okay because at least I know I am securely in my needed exit lane. Do humans really drive this way? Some do, many do not. What's actually more likely is that I'll "procrastinate" and put off getting into the slow lane until the last moment, just in time to make that exit.

This is more efficient driving, from the perspective of most drivers (I realize that you traffic researchers out there would argue that this is lousy driving and worsens traffic, and it is unsafe driving, but anyway that's a different debate for another day).

We are building "procrastination" into the AI of self-driving cars. Rather than being the goody two shoes kind of driver, our view is that if self-driving cars are supposed to be able ultimately drive as good as a human, they should be adopting human driving techniques. The utopians out there are going to go ape, since they believe that all AI self-driving cars will be perfectly civil and obey all laws and be sweet and kind to all other cars on the roads. Maybe. I don't think so.

Don't misjudge what I am saying. We are not intending to make AI self-driving cars that are daredevils. This might end-up happening, but that's not what we are designing. Our focus is AI self-driving cars that drive as reasonable humans do. There are many driving situations wherein "procrastination" (the good kind) is actually handy to consider as part of the driving repertoire. Shouldn't be used all the time. Shouldn't be used indiscriminately. Should be used in the right situation, at the right time, in the right way.

Some want us to achieve AI self-driving cars that can pass a variation of the Turing Test. This means that AI self-driving cars would be able to drive a car in the same manner that a human does. If we were standing outside and watching two cars drive along, and we couldn't see into the cars, and we had to try and say which one was being driven by the human and which by the AI – if we couldn't discern which was which, in a small way the AI has passed a type of Turing Test.

Today's AI self-driving cars are programmed to drive a car like a teenage novice driver. This is not going to get us to the vaunted Level 5, which is a true AI self-driving car. Using the technique of purposeful "procrastination" is one of the many ways in which an AI self-driving car can drive more like a human can. Say, I avoided doing more development on the machine learning algorithm for our AI system because I opted to instead write this -- I guess that was my "procrastination" act for the day.

CHAPTER 5

NTSB REPORT
AND
TESLA CAR CRASH

Lance B. Eliot

CHAPTER 5

NTSB REPORT AND

TESLA CAR CRASH

Based on the June 7, 2018 release of the preliminary NTSB report about the fatal car crash of a Tesla on March 23, 2018, I provide in today's column an initial forensic analysis of the incident.

Keep in mind that the just released NTSB report (about three days ago as of the writing of this) is very slim on details at this juncture of the investigation and so there really isn't much in terms of facts and evidence that would allow for a thorough analysis. Nonetheless, it is instructive to be able to try and piece together the clues released to-date and see if useful insights can be gleaned.

Faithful readers of my online columns will recall that I had done a similar forensic analysis of the Uber self-driving car incident that occurred in Arizona, and that later on, upon release of the initial report by the NTSB, it turns out that my predictions of what likely occurred were quite prescient. Indeed, there didn't seem to be any other published news item about the incident at the time that had so aptly predicted what might have taken place.

Learning From the "Past"

At the Cybernetic AI Self-Driving Car Institute, we are developing AI systems for self-driving cars. As a result, we are keenly interested in what happens in incidents involving self-driving cars, along with

81

wanting to provide insights for auto makers and other tech firms that are in the midst of developing and maintaining such AI systems.

As per the famous quote of philosopher George Santayana: "Those who cannot remember the past are condemned to repeat it." With the rapid advances taking place with AI self-driving cars, and with the use of our public roadways as part of a grand experiment to see whether self-driving cars are viable, it is especially crucial that we all look at every morsel of what is taking place and try to as rapidly as possible consider what action is most appropriate to ensure the safety of us all. Our collective desire as a society to have AI self-driving cars needs to be balanced by our collective desire to be reasonably safe on our public roadways too.

For some of you, you might say that the risks of any self-driving car endangerment are simply the presumed calculated risk of the person that has opted to drive such a car. This though is narrow thinking and does not include the proper larger scope. The human driver is certainly taking a risk, but so too would any occupants in the car that are accompanying the car with the human driver – suppose the driver has children in the car, are those children able to also calculate the risks involved? The self-driving car could ram into and injure or kill humans that are in other nearby cars – did they get a chance to assess and take on the risks of that self-driving car? Pedestrians could be injured or killed – did they have a say in accepting the risks of the self-driving car?

I mention this because at some of my presentations around the country there are at times self-driving car pundits that stand-up and say that it should be each person's own choice as to whether or not they want to drive a self-driving car, and that the government and anyone else should stay out of it. If the driver of a self-driving car was able to drive the car in a manner that was completely isolated from all of the rest of us, I likely would agree that it could be an informed personal decision to make.

We must though keep in mind that driving on our public roadways is a societal interaction and therefore would seemingly be a societal decision. It is for this reason that driving by humans is deemed a "privilege" and not a "right" per se. The Department of Motor Vehicles (DMV) in most states lays out what a human driver must do and not do, in order to retain the privilege to drive a car on our public roadways. There isn't an irrevocable right to drive on our public roadways. It's a revocable privilege.

Context of the Tesla Incident

Here's some key aspects about the Tesla incident, based on using the NTSB preliminary report, which noted this:

- Accident Location: Mountain View , CA
- Accident Date: 4/23/2018
- Accident ID: HWY18FH011
- Date Adopted: 6/7/2018
- NTSB Number: HWY18FH011 Preliminary

On a relatively sunny and dry day in California on Friday, March 23, 2018, in the morning around 9:30 a.m. PDT a Tesla Model X P100D 2017 was being driven southbound on the multi-lane US Highway 101 (US-101) in Mountain View and was nearing the interchange with the State Highway 85 (SH-85). This is a typical California type of interchange that involves various paths to get onto each of the two intersecting major highways. Drivers can choose to go from the US-101 onto the SH-85, and drivers that are on the SH-85 can choose to go onto the US-101. Both of these highways are very commonly driven and typically popular with traffic, especially on a Friday morning.

Notice that I've mentioned some important aspects already. Was the incident occurring on a rainy day? No. It was sunny and the roads were dry. This is important because we might otherwise need to consider the weather as a factor in what occurred. I think it is relatively sound to assume that weather was not a factor since the roads were dry and it was sunny. Was it nighttime or daytime when the incident occurred? It was daytime, and nearing mid-morning, and so it would have been relatively well lit.

I mention this because if it were say nighttime, we'd need to consider the impact of darkness and how it could have diminished the capability of the cameras used for the self-driving car.

Were the roads involved somewhat obscure or more commonly used? Answer, they were commonly used. This did not occur in some back-country location. These were modern day highways. They are well paved and well maintained. They are multi-lane in shape and not single lanes. Traffic is relatively abundant on these highways. If it was the same time on a Sunday, I'd bet that there would have been a lot less traffic. Friday morning is around the time that many drivers are going to work and so it would have been a generally busy highway, along with generally busy in terms of cars trying to use the interchange to get to where they needed to go.

You might wonder why I am laboring to mention these nuances. I hope that you'll see the "magic" behind doing a forensic analysis. It is crucial to consider each piece of evidence and try to use it for putting together the puzzle. This involves considering what we do know, what we can use as leverage to speculate about, and also what we know to not be the case – for example, we know it was not snowing. This then rules out that somehow snow might have been a factor in the incident. Now, since it essentially never snows in Mountain View, I suppose you might say its kind of ridiculous that I point out it wasn't snowing, but it is as important to point out what we can about any factors that might come to play. Not everyone knows that it doesn't snow in Mountain View and it could be that some reading this would wonder whether say snow or rain or other conditions came to play.

The Tesla at the time of the incident was in the High Occupancy Vehicle (HOV) lane, which was the second lane from the left of the median that divides the southbound and northbound lanes. Normally it is permitted to travel in the HOV lane when you have multiple occupants, while in this case there was a solo driver, but since the Tesla is an electric car it qualifies to go in the HOV. The human driver was a 38-year-old male and sadly he died as a result of the crash. There isn't any detail yet in the NTSB preliminary report about the driver, but for this herein analysis let's assume that he was versed in driving the Tesla, and that he had likely gone this way before, and that he was familiar with the nature of the Tesla driving controls. We don't know that any of this is the case, so please keep in mind that it is for the moment an assumption.

The NTSB indicates they have examined "performance data downloaded from the vehicle." What we don't yet know is what this actually means. Did the Tesla have an Event Data Recorder (EDR)? This EDR is a so-called black box that is akin to the black box that are used in airplanes and helpful when determining why an airplane crashed. Or, did the NTSB have to get various memory dumps from other processors in the Tesla, and if so, which ones and what ones weren't available perhaps due to being destroyed or damaged? Has the NTSB gotten access to data that would have been transmitted potentially to the Tesla cloud that allows for OTA (Over The Air) updates? We don't yet know the depth and extent of the data that the NTSB has collected or intends to collect.

The Crash Itself

The NTSB report indicates that the Tesla was going at about 71 miles per hour when it struck the tail-end of a concrete median that had a "crash attenuator" as an additional barrier at its leading edge. You've probably seen these attenuators before and yet didn't know they had a name. It is a special kind of barrier that is setup to help try and "soften" the blow of a car that crashes into the finger-point of a concrete median. Years ago, traffic studies showed that when cars hit directly a concrete median at the edge point, it pretty much is like slicing bread with a knife. Thus, the thought was to put something at the edge that would dampen the blow. In some cases, you'll see those bright yellow barrels that are filled with sand or sometimes water. The attenuator used in this instance is specially built for the purpose of sitting at the edge and taking the blow of a car, along with trying to warn a car to not hit it, doing so by having yellow and black markings to visibly suggest don't hit it.

What's an interesting added twist is that the NTSB report says that the attenuator had been previously damaged. It would be helpful if the NTSB could say more about this. Was the attenuator so damaged that it could no longer perform as intended? Suppose it was damaged to the extent that it could no longer soften the blow of a crash, or maybe could only do so to the degree of say 50%? This is important to know as part of whether or not the crash might have led to survivability or not. Also, was the painted or marked aspect of the attenuator still visible and fully presented, or was it damaged such that the attenuator was no longer sufficiently able to suggest the don't hit me indication?

This could be crucial for both human drivers as to whether they could discern that it was a crash-warning attenuator, and in this case perhaps even more so crucial since the question is whether the Tesla cameras and vision processing could discern it.

I mention this aspect since by-and-large humans are generally able to visually figure out when they see an attenuator that is indeed an attenuator, and humans have the "common sense" that it is there to safe lives and that if you are driving toward it you are likely making a big mistake because it is there when behind it is something fierce like a concrete median. Did the camera of the Tesla capture images of the attenuator? Did the AI system examine the images and detect that within the image was an attenuator? We don't yet know, since the NTSB report doesn't say anything about this.

It is possible that the Tesla AI system has used machine learning to try and determine what attenuators look like. This can be done via the use of artificial neural networks that are trained on thousands and thousands of images of attenuators. Generally, one would like to assume that the Tesla AI has been trained sufficiently to recognize an attenuator, but suppose that this one was damaged in such a way that it no longer well-matched the training images? It is conceivable that the AI system did not thusly categorize the attenuator as an attenuator, and might have classified it as some unknown object, if it detected it at all.

Something else about that damaged attenuator is worth mentioning. According to the NTSB report, the attenuator was damaged on March 12, 2018 by a crash involving a Toyota Prius 2010. The attenuator, which the NTSB report says was an SCI smart cushion attenuator system, one might ask why it had not been repaired as yet? The Tesla incident happened on March 23, 2018. That's about 11 days or nearly two weeks since it was first damaged on March 12, 2018. Was it scheduled to be repaired or replaced? Again, we don't know that it would have made a difference, but it would be something that the NTSB will hopefully report on.

The NTSB report does not indicate what kind of sensors were used on this particular Tesla Model X. It would be crucial for the NTSB to indicate what sensors were used, and also whether it was known as to whether or not the sensors were in working order at the time leading up to the crash. We don't yet know.

I am going to guess that it might have had these sensors (please don't hold me to this, it is just an educated guess based on what normally would be included):

- Rearward Looking Side Cameras: 100 meters (about 328 feet)
- Wide Forward Camera: 60 meters (about 197 feet)
- Main Forward Camera: 150 meters (about 492 feet)
- Narrow Forward Camera: 250 meters (about 820 feet)
- Rear View Camera: 50 meters (about 164 feet)
- Ultrasonic: 8 meters (about 26 feet)
- Forward Looking Side Camera: 80 meters (about 262 feet)
- Radar: 160 meters (about 524 feet)

I've also indicated the typical ranges of the considered maximum detection for each of those devices. This is important to know since the analysis of a crash involves determining how many feet or meters away could the AI system have potentially detected something. In the case of the Uber incident in Arizona, I had used the reported speed of the car to then try to ascertain how far in-advance of the crash could the AI have potentially detected the object in the roadway (it was a pedestrian walking a bicycle). Knowing the type of sensors and their detection ranges is vital to such an analysis.

The Counterclockwise Spin

Per the NTSB report for the Mountain View incident, the report says that the Tesla struck the attenuator while going 71 mile per hour, and then the impact "rotated the Tesla counterclockwise" and ultimately "caused a separation of the front portion of the vehicle." I think we can all agree that hitting something like the attenuator at a speed of 71 miles per hour is going to exert a tremendous amount of force and it certainly seems to have been the case since it caused the front of the Tesla to become separated. It was a hard hit. I don't think anyone can dispute that.

What's interesting is the notion that the Tesla spun counterclockwise. I've not yet seen anyone comment about this aspect. I'll speculate about it. If the Tesla had hit the attenuator fully head-on, we would need to study the physics of the result, but it generally might not have led to a spin of the Tesla. More than likely, the Tesla probably hit at a front-edge of the car, such as toward the left side of the front edge or to the right of the front edge. This would be more likely to generate a spinning action after the impact. Since the Tesla apparently spun counterclockwise, we'll assume for the moment that it hit at the left side edge of the front of the Tesla, which then jammed the left side against the attenuator, and the right side of the Tesla continued forward which caused it to pivot from the leftside, making it go counterclockwise. This is all speculation and we'll need to see what the NTSB has to say about it.

I'll explain in a moment why I think this counterclockwise spinning is a useful clue.

Aftermath of the Crash

After having crashed and spun, the Tesla was involved in subsequent collisions involving two other cars that were presumably driving southbound and got inadvertently caught up in the incident. I'll assume for now that those additional crashes had nothing to do with the initial crash per se, and were just part of the aftermath.

I am saddened that those subsequent crashes occurred, and it also serves as a reminder about my earlier remarks that incidents involving self-driving cars aren't necessarily confined to impacting just the driver but can also include other innocents that get caught up in the cascading impacts. According to the NTSB report, one of those other drivers suffered minor injuries, and the other was uninjured. I'd say that's nearly a miracle. No matter what led to the initial crash, any aftermath can often be horrific.

The NTSB report further mentions that the 400-volt lithium-ion high-voltage battery in the Tesla caught fire as it was breached during the incident, and a post-crash fire ensued (these can be intense fires; the fire department arrived and was able to put out the fire). It is uplifting to note that the NTSB report essentially suggests that bystanders got out of their cars and came to the rescue of the driver in the Tesla, bravely removing him from the vehicle, in spite of the dangers of the fire. The NTSB report indicates that the Tesla driver was transported to a hospital but died there from his injuries. In any case, I applaud those brave souls that rescued him from the crash.

Layout of the Crash Scene

The NTSB preliminary report does not depict a layout of the crash scene. I've used Google Maps to try and see if I can figure out what the crash scene was like. This is admittedly speculation. The final NTSB report should officially describe the crash scene and will be usually based on photos taken at the time and physical evidence at the crash scene, as per the investigative team that inspected the location.

Based on what I can discern, it appears that the crash occurred at the split of the US-101 continuing forward and an exit ramp to get onto the SH-85 as a left-side offshoot. There appears to be a triangular shaped "gore area" that divides the two. I'm sure you've seen this kind of thing before. You have two lanes that are running next to each other, and at some point up ahead they split from each other. At that splitting or fork, one lane goes straight ahead, while the other veers off. In-between the split is a triangular area that divides the two splitting lanes. In this case, there was a concrete median in that gore area and it had the attenuator at the front-edge of the concrete median.

It appears that there was for a while two HOV lanes leading up to the split. One HOV lane was for those continuing on US-101, and the other was for those cars wanting to veer off to the left as part of the exit from the US-101 leading to the SH-85. I don't know that this is exactly where the incident occurred. As I say, I've just looked at Google Maps and tried to guess based on what the NTSB slim details so far suggest.

See Figure 1.

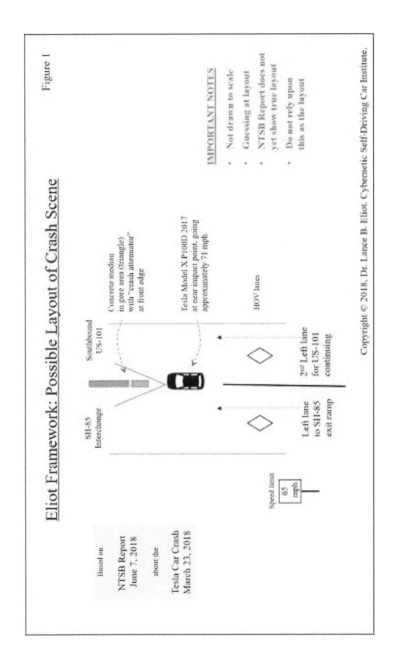

Eliot Framework: Possible Layout of Crash Scene

Figure 1

IMPORTANT NOTES

* Not drawn to scale
* Guessing at layout
* NTSB Report does not yet show true layout
* Do not rely upon this as the layout

Concrete median in gore area (triangle) with "crash attenuator" at front edge

Tesla Model X P100D 2017 at near impact point, going approximately 71 mph

Southbound US-101

SH-85 Interchange

HOV lanes

2nd Left lane for US-101 continuing

Left lane to SH-85 exit ramp

Speed limit
65 mph

Based on

NTSB Report June 7, 2018

about the

Tesla Car Crash March 23, 2018

Timing of the Crash

The vital aspects about the crash are contained in the timing aspects reported so far by the NTSB.

According to the NTSB, at 18 minutes 55 seconds before the crash, the Autopilot was engaged. It apparently remained engaged the entire time thereafter. This is important because if the Autopilot was not engaged then we likely wouldn't be discussing any of this, it would generally have been a traditional crash since the Tesla would have been operating like any everyday car. Also, if the Autopilot had suddenly been engaged just seconds before the crash, we might be of a mind to say that the Autopilot had insufficient time to get started and so it was not especially a participant in the crash. In this case, it seems like the Autopilot had been on, it had been on for quite some time before the crash, and it was still on at the time of the crash.

Take a look at Figure 2.

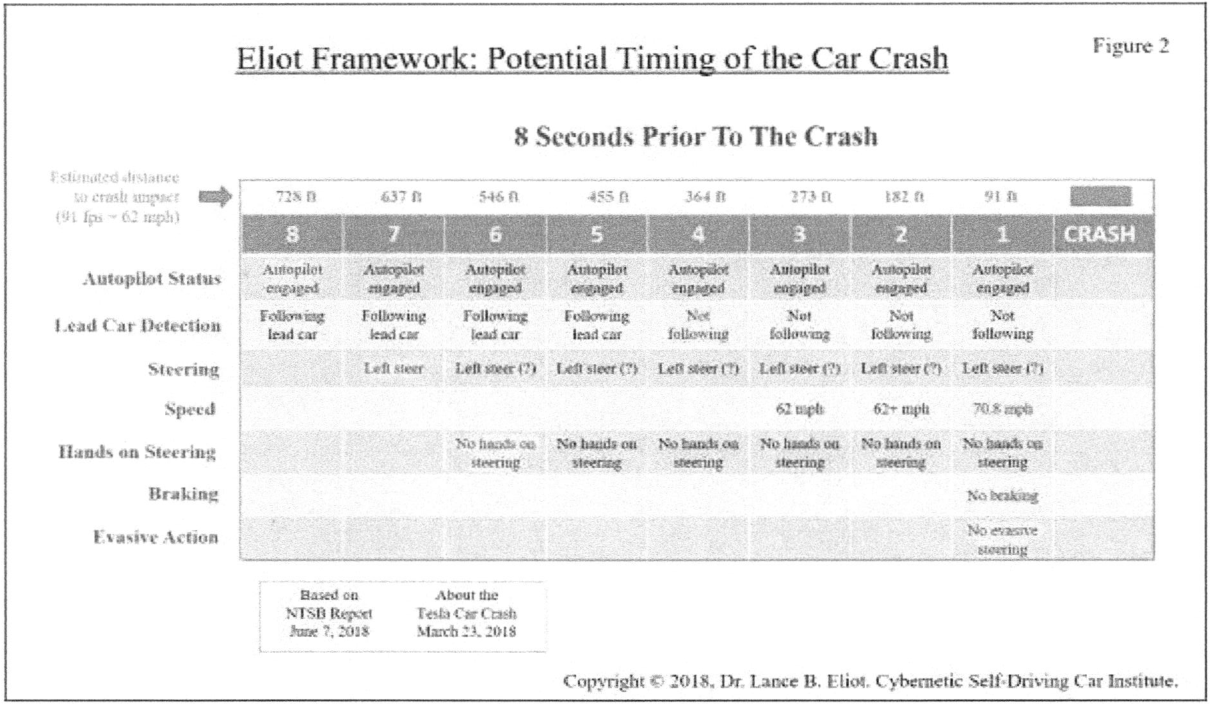

Figure 2

Eliot Framework: Potential Timing of the Car Crash

8 Seconds Prior To The Crash

Estimated distance to crash impact (91 fps ~ 62 mph)	728 ft	637 ft	546 ft	455 ft	364 ft	273 ft	182 ft	91 ft	CRASH
	8	7	6	5	4	3	2	1	
Autopilot Status	Autopilot engaged	Autopilot engaged	Autopilot engaged	Autopilot engaged	Autopilot engaged	Autopilot engaged	Autopilot engaged	Autopilot engaged	
Lead Car Detection	Following lead car	Following lead car	Following lead car	Following lead car	Not following	Not following	Not following	Not following	
Steering		Left steer	Left steer (?)	Left steer (?)	Left steer (?)	Left steer (?)	Left steer (?)	Left steer (?)	
Speed						62 mph	62+ mph	70.8 mph	
Hands on Steering			No hands on steering	No hands on steering	No hands on steering	No hands on steering	No hands on steering	No hands on steering	
Braking								No braking	
Evasive Action								No evasive steering	

Based on NTSB Report June 7, 2018

About the Tesla Car Crash March 23, 2018

The Tesla was reportedly following a lead car, doing so at 8 seconds before the crash (and might have been doing so even longer, but we don't yet know), and at 4 seconds before the crash it was no longer following a lead car. For those of you not familiar with self-driving cars, they often use a pied piper approach to driving. They spot a car ahead, and then try to match to the pace of that car. If the car ahead speeds-up, the self-driving car will speed-up, but only to some maximum such as the speed limit or perhaps what has been set on the cruise control via the human driver in the self-driving car. If the car ahead slows down, the self-driving car tends to slow down.

As I've said many times before, this pied piper approach is extremely simplistic. It's what a teenage novice driver does when they are first learning to drive, but they quickly realize there are many downsides to this approach. If the approach is not augmented by more sophisticated driving techniques, it's something that has only limited utility. By the way, keep in mind that the Tesla models of today are considered at a Level 2 or Level 3, but are not yet at a true Level 5, which is a self-driving car for which the AI can entirely drive the car without any human intervention. At the levels less than 5, the human driver is considered the driver of the car, in spite of whatever else the "self-driving car" can do or is suggested or implied that it can do.

Once the lead car was no longer ahead of the Tesla, the Tesla then reportedly increased speed, since it was going at 62 miles per hour while following the lead car, and then with a presumed clear space ahead it opted to increase speed to 71 miles per hour at the time of the crash. This "makes sense" in that the system will aim to go to the maximum allowed speed if it believes that there is no car ahead of it that would impede doing so. The NTSB says that the driver had set the cruise control to a maximum of 75 miles per hour, and so the Tesla was likely trying to accelerate to that stated speed. As a side note, the NTSB points out that the speed limit in that location is only 65 miles per hour.

What's especially intriguing in the NTSB preliminary report is that supposedly the Tesla was left steering, doing so at 7 seconds before the crash. The implication is that this continued until the actual crash.

What was causing the Tesla to left steer? We aren't sure that it was the human driver, since the NTSB says that there weren't any hands on the steering wheel at 6 seconds to go, and nor until the crash. We also don't know how much left steering was involved – was it a radical left or just a mild torque to the left? We really need to see what the NTSB final report says about this.

Per the NTSB, there was no pre-crash braking by the Tesla. This implies that neither the human driver hit the brakes, and nor did the Autopilot system. Per the NTSB, there was no evasive steering. This implies that neither the human driver tried to steer clear of the crash, and nor did the Autopilot system.

This then is the conundrum.

We have a car going about 70 miles per hour that plowed into the gore area and unabatedly slammed into the attenuator that was at the end of the concrete median and did so without any apparent indication by the behavior of the car that it was about to happen.

The human driver did not try to stop the car. The human driver did not try to avoid the attenuator by swerving the car. Any of these options were presumably available in that we can assume reasonably that the brakes were operational and that the steering wheel was operational, as far as we know.

The Autopilot system did not try to stop the car. The Autopilot system did not try to avoid the attenuator by swerving the car. Any of these options were presumably available in that we can assume reasonably that the brakes were operational and that the steering was operational and that the Autopilot system had an ability to command those controls, as far as we know.

Before I launch into speculation about how this occurred, let's add some other elements to the situation. The speed of 62 miles per hour is about the same as going 91 feet per second. The speed of 71 miles per hour is about the same as going 104 feet per second. The usual rule-of-thumb for proper driving practices is to maintain a distance of about 1 car length for every 10 miles per hour of speed. Most human drivers don't do this, and they often are very unsafe in terms of the distance they maintain from a car ahead of them. In any case, most self-driving car systems try to maintain the proper recommended distance.

The Tesla Model X is approximately 16 feet in length. So, going at about 60 miles per hour, it presumably was trying to maintain a distance of about (60 mph / 10) x 16 = 96 feet, or 6 car lengths. In the timeline, this would mean that the Tesla was about one second behind the lead car.

Where did the lead car go? Did it opt to get out of the HOV lane and maybe went into the lane to the right? In which case, this implies that in one second of time, from 5 seconds out to the 4 seconds out, it changed lanes and got into the next lane over. Or, did it maybe switch into the exit ramp lane to the left? We don't know.

Or, did the Tesla move to the left from the 7 seconds out to the 4 seconds out, using up 3 seconds, moving so much so that it was no longer directly in the HOV lane that it had been using to follow the lead car? Thus, the lead car never made any lane change, and it was instead the Tesla that essentially did so, and therefore it no longer detected the lead car that was in the prior HOV lane that the Tesla had been presumably squarely in.

It could be that the Tesla was shifting to the left and ended-up not yet being fully in the exit ramp lane, and nor any longer fully in the ongoing HOV lane. It was in-between. Suppose it had not yet fully ended-up in the exit ramp to the left, and then struck the attenuator at the left side of the front of the Tesla. This fits with the aspect earlier that the Tesla then did a counterclockwise spin (I told you that I'd bring this back into the analysis).

Have you ever been in your car on a highway and couldn't decide whether to take an exit or continue forward, and you began to straddle both options, which ultimately would mean that you'd ram into whatever was sitting between the two options? I'm guessing you've done this before. And, sweated like mad afterwards that you cut things so close as to making the decision of which path to take.

In this case, one scenario is that the Tesla was following a lead car, and for which this seemed perfectly normal and common, and then with just a few seconds before impact with the attenuator, and for reasons yet unknown, the Tesla began to shift to the left, as though it was going to get out of the existing HOV lane and into the exit ramp lane but did so without sufficient urgency.

Did the Autopilot intend to actively switch lanes?

Or, did it somehow lose itself in terms of the markings on the roadway and it was unsure of where the lane really was?

Why didn't the human driver take over the controls and do something? One explanation is that with only about 3 seconds left to go, which is the point at which the Tesla was apparently no longer following the lead car, the human driver might not have had sufficient time to realize what was happening. Up until then, perhaps the human driver was watching the car ahead and assumed that as long as the car ahead was ahead, it was safe to continue allowing the Autopilot to drive the car.

Was the human driver paying attention to the road? Maybe yes, maybe no – we don't know. The NTSB says that for the 60 seconds before the crash, the human driver put their hands on the steering wheel on 3 occasions for a total of 34 seconds. This implies that within that last minute, the human driver possibly was paying attention to the driving task.

The Tesla has a steering wheel touch indicator, but does not have a eye tracking capability and nor a facial tracking capability. These are aspects that some industry experts have asked about and which in this case could have provided further info about the situation.

Why didn't the Tesla detect the attenuator?

In other words, even if the Tesla somehow was veering to the left, whether due to the human driver or due to the Autopilot itself, presumably the Autopilot should have still been able to detect that there was an attenuator up ahead and that the Tesla was heading straight for it.

There are a multitude of possibilities to explain this.

It could be that on this sunny morning that the sun was in a position that caused glare and that the cameras on the Tesla could not get a clear enough image to detect the attenuator.

You might say that even if that happened, the forward-facing radar should have detected the attenuator.

Was the attenuator so low to the ground and positioned that the radar couldn't get a solid radar return?

Or, could it be that the damaged attenuator made it less likely to be spotted by radar?

Another possibility is that the camera was reporting that it didn't see anything ahead, and let's pretend the radar was saying there was something ahead, but suppose the AI system is coded in a manner that it needs to have both agree in order to take action. It might be that it was programmed that if the radar says be wary, but if the camera does not agree, then the car continues ahead and waits until the two will concur. This is sometimes done to avoid ghosts that appear falsely either on the radar or on the visual processing. Presumably, the AI should not take overt action if it is not "abundantly" the case that action is needed.

In this case, it could be that the no action was taken under the assumption by the system that no action was better than taking the wrong action. In hindsight, we of course would say that the system should have taken evasive action, even if it only had partial indication about what was ahead, but this is only speculation about the events that transpired.

It is noteworthy too that the lead car was no longer ahead at the 4 second mark. This means that the time that the Tesla system had to presumably spot the attenuator was perhaps only with about 4 seconds left to go. To some degree, the camera images and the radar could have been blocked by the lead car. With the "sudden" appearance of the attenuator, there is another possible explanation for the situation.

One further scenario is that the Tesla system ran out of time.

Suppose that it really did get solid images of the attenuator, and that it got solid radar. The question arises as to how much time is needed by the Autopilot to digest this information and then take action.

Here's the standard framework of stages for a self-driving car:
- o   Sensor Data Collection
- o   Sensor Fusion Analysis
- o   Virtual World Model Updating
- o   AI Action Plan Updating
- o   Car Controls Commands

Suppose with 4 seconds left to impact, the sensor data collection took a chunk of that time. Then, assume that the sensor fusion of combining the sensor data took a chunk of that time, including maybe wrestling with a difference of opinion by the camera images versus the radar. Then, the virtual world model had to be updated to reflect the surroundings. Then, an AI action plan had to be updated as to what steps to next take in terms of the driving of the car. Finally, there is a chunk of time involved in issuing car controls commands and having the car respond and abide by the commands.

One aspect is that the Autopilot used up the available time and was in the midst of determining what to do. Perhaps it was going to take perhaps 5 seconds to figure out what to do and enact an evasive maneuver, but with just 4 seconds until impact it was too late by the time it figured out what action to take.

Awaiting the NTSB Final Report

Until the NTSB provides more details in subsequent reports about the incident, we're all in the dark about what actually happened.

In this analysis, I've opted to not get mired into the ongoing debate about who is responsible for the acts of a self-driving car in these kinds of incidents. As Tesla has made very clear, their view is that the human driver is ultimately responsible for the driving of the Tesla cars: "Autopilot is intended for use only with a fully attentive driver," furthermore it "does not prevent all accidents – such a standard would be impossible – but it makes them much less likely to occur."

I've written and spoken many times about the issue of the notion that self-driving cars and their human drivers are co-sharing responsibility. It's something as a society we need to carefully consider.

For those of you that are interested in these kinds of self-driving car crash analyses, I'll be updating my analysis once there is more reporting by the NTSB about this incident. The end result will hopefully make us all aware of the potential limitations of self-driving cars and allow us all as a society to make further informed decisions about what we expect of them. This also should aid auto makers and tech firms in determining what kind of safety aspects they should be including in their AI systems and how to try and make self-driving cars as safe as feasible.

CHAPTER 6

START OVER AI
AND
SELF-DRIVING CARS

CHAPTER 6

START OVER AI
AND SELF-DRIVING CARS

When my daughter was quite young, we would go over to a nearby playground and she would gleefully enjoy going on the swings and the slides. One day, it had been raining, and so we went over to the playground but everything seemed too wet to play on. She noticed though that there was a little stream of water making its way across the playground, being driven by the leftover rain water on the grass that was draining along the now-made stream and flowing out to the street.

She decided to pick a particular spot along the small stream, and began to make a tiny bridge made from twigs that were on the ground. This seemed like a quite inventive way to turn our otherwise rained-out visit to the playground into something fun to do. I watched in fascination as she tried to hook together twigs and make them into an arch over the inches-wide stream of rain water. At her young age, this seemed like quite a mental feat in that she had to discern how to intertwine the twigs, how to try and arch them over the water, and do so without having the structure fall into the stream itself.

Well, it turns out that the structure became top heavy and collapsed into the stream. Away went most of the twigs. I thought she might get upset or at least stand-up and walk away in disgust. Instead, she pondered the result of her efforts. For about a solid minute, she looked at the stream, she looked at the twigs, she looked around the playground, and was lost in deep thought. I had no idea what she might

103

be thinking. Suddenly snapping into action, she went over and collected some scattered tree branches that had fallen during the storm, and also got other of nature's leftovers such as fallen leaves. She then began to build anew a bridge across that stream. This version was going to likely last a thousand years.

It was exciting to see that she had the tenacity to continue her quest. She did not give up. She reviewed what had occurred and carefully analyzed the situation. She re-examined the resources available to her. She re-planned what to do next. She carried out her plan. For a small child, these are wonderful signs of thoughtfulness and mindfulness. As you can imagine, I was elated to think that this was a precursor to what she would become as an adult. Indeed, this is how she turned out!

Anchors Can Weigh Us Down

Why did I tell this story? Sometimes, we need to start over. It could be a system that you are coding at work and it has reached a point that there seems to be a dead end. Or, maybe you have a home project that has gotten bent out of shape. You could try to continue with what you started, but at times this can be worse than just starting over. When you build upon something already started, you often need to bend over backwards to make the new stuff fit. You become anchored to what was already done. If the already done aspects are not very good, you can become trapped and mired in what was there before.

It's the curse of the legacy.

Whether it is just because it exists, or sometimes due to tradition, or for whatever reason, the past can cause our future to become pinched. Meanwhile, someone else comes along and sees a new future, and so they jump past the old ways. Some would say that Uber did this in the taxi business. The taxi business was mired in the old ways, you had to call to get a taxi, the taxi was often dirty and ugly, the driver was difficult to deal with, etc. Uber opted to skip past the conventional taxi and use a new form of taxi, everyday people driving in their everyday cars, and which you could contact via an app on your smartphone. It was a jump that many at the time thought was crazy. They weren't the only ones to see a different future, and so I want to make clear they alone did not have this vision, but nonetheless they were able to carry it out in a substantial way.

Let's revisit this whole notion about starting over and recast it into the field of Artificial Intelligence (AI).

In an earlier era of the AI field, there was a great deal of fanfare and mania about so-called expert systems, sometimes also referred to as knowledge-based systems or rules-based systems. There was an entire sub-industry that sprang up to provide automated tools for knowledge acquisition, for knowledge encoding, and so on. The hope at the time was that this was the breakthrough towards building true AI systems that could exhibit intelligence and intelligent behavior.

Though there was a lot accomplished during that era, it eventually became more apparent that it was not going to get us to the true sense of AI. Some of you might recall my writings and speeches from that era that said as such, and for which I cautioned that we shouldn't be jumping the gun on what expert systems would ultimately gain us. For some people, they now say that we went from the AI spring to the AI winter, wherein after a let-down of expert systems there was a sense that we were still a long ways from true AI.

During the expert systems heyday, there was also some action in the machine learning realm. The use of artificial neural networks was just beginning to come out of the research labs. Most of the neural networks were being built as prototypes. They were relatively small in size. Just a handful of layers. The number of neurons would number maybe in the hundreds at most. The mathematical properties were still being developed and explored. Tools to build neural networks tended to be clumsy and awkward to use. It was pretty much an arcane part of the AI field.

The grand convergence of lower cost processors, higher performance processing, ready access to large data sets, and other factors then prompted artificial neural networks to regain attention. And, indeed, it has become the darling of the AI field. Seemingly impressive feats involving vision processing. Used for doing foreign language translation. Winning at games such as Go. Etc.

Generally, most that are in-the-know would agree that these artificial neural networks are not a breakthrough in the sense that it has yet to be shown that this approach will lead us to truly intelligent systems. They are an incremental advance and appear to provide progress forward.

Where in this is the ability to exhibit common sense?

Where in this is the "spark" that we consider the nature of human intelligence?

Is It Just Scale Or Something More

There are proponents of the artificial neural network approach that say we just haven't hit scale as yet. We have some seemingly large-scale neural networks involving thousands upon thousands of artificial neurons. But, the human brain is estimated to have 100 billion neurons, and an estimated 100 trillion connections.

No man-made artificial neural network yet approaches that magnitude. The question many are asking is whether if we can actually create an artificial neural network of that same size, will we suddenly have ourselves a functioning mind?

In essence, if you have two things that are about the same size, one a biological embodiment and the other some kind of machine or automation embodiment, will the machine version then be as capable as the biological version?

We don't know, but we do know that the way in which we are simulating neurons in an artificial neural network is not the same as the biological implementation in an actual brain, and so already we have the aspect of a difference between the two. Presumably, the artificial one being inherently inferior just by the "mechanics" of things alone, and so right away one might doubt the efficacy of by sheer size of counts of neurons and connections alone that this simulated approach will be unlikely to rise to the same pinnacle.

Even if we could get the housing to be the same, what about the contents?

Indeed, there is belief that the human brain is more than just a bucket of neurons and connections. There is perhaps some kind of pre-wiring and pre-setup that makes this collection of Lego's into something special that can ultimately showcase intelligence. If that's the case, we need to somehow get our artificial version to become more like that. Or, we can hope that perhaps there is more than one way to skin a cat, meaning that maybe we can achieve intelligence but do so via some other means than the approach that we are aware of today (the wetware brain).

Are we though maybe trapped already in our ways?

For the artificial neural networks of today, we need to present them with sometimes millions of data instances to get them to pattern onto something. Want to be able to find cats in photos, first run millions of cat photos into the neural network for training purposes. You might then get a good "cat" image detector. But, it is possible that with just a few pixel changes, you could present to the trained neural network an image that does contain a cat, and for which a human would detect it, but for which the neural network might not.

Neural networks as we know them so far are brittle. They also require an immense amount of training data samples. They are very narrow in their focus.

Does a small child need to look at millions of cat images to figure out what a cat looks like? Don't think so. How does a small child know what a cat looks like, if they haven't seen millions or even thousands of cats to pattern after? Somehow, the small child accomplishes such a feat. No one knows how.

There has been a long time assumption that the human brain when a baby is first born contains nothing much in it. It is pretty much devoid of what we consider knowledge. Then, as the baby encounters the world around them, the brain soaks in the information and begins to formulate intelligence. In a seemingly magical way, the baby increases in intelligence and becomes a child, and the child gradually increases in intelligence and becomes the adult.

Is indeed the baby's brain a true blank slate? Is it simply a collection of neurons that are empty and then become formulated as the intelligence fermentation process gets underway?

There are cognitive scientists that would say that even the youngest baby has some form of neural wiring that provides them with an innate ability to do things like object representation, they have an approximate number sense for counting purposes, they have some kind of geometric navigation built-in, they have something that enables their use of language, and so on. We might not be able to communicate with a young baby per se, since their language skills and motor skills don't readily allow it, but nonetheless inside that head is pre-wiring that already out-the-gate gives that human a huge step towards intelligence.

It would be as though we made sure that every artificial neural network started-up with an underlying structure and content that was essential for moving forward. A kind of bootstrap as it were. It would be an "innate" capability and allow that neural network to go beyond some narrow focus of only being able to play the game Go or detect the image of a cat.

But, we don't have anything remotely like that as yet.

This then returns me to my story about how my daughter took a look at the fallen twigs and stepped back to re-think how to solve the problem at hand. In the machine learning realm, maybe we should be putting our efforts towards figuring out the bootstrap. Until we have that figured out, the rest of this stuff that we are doing with neural networks might be essentially for not. We are trying to use the neural network structures that we know today, and building upon that to get towards intelligence.

Maybe, we are building in a manner that requires a redo. Is there a means to develop the innate core, and once we've nailed that, the rest of what we want to accomplish will be stepwise and come to us like so many dominos that fall one after another?

AI Self-Driving Cars Reboot

What does this have to do with AI self-driving cars?

At the Cybernetic AI Self-Driving Car Institute, we are pursuing both the conventional approach towards developing AI self-driving cars, and we are simultaneously pursuing the "outlier" notion that the only way we might really get to a true AI self-driving car is by a more radical approach to doing so.

Let's suppose that all the auto makers and tech firms that are trying to create AI to achieve true Level 5 self-driving cars are not quite able to achieve it. We all keep pushing the existing approaches of machine learning as we know it today, we keep putting in faster and faster processors, and yet we don't get to the true Level 5. A true Level 5 is a self-driving car that can do whatever driving that a human can do, and not need any human intervention.

Maybe we get to a Level 5 self-driving car that's pretty good, and seems to cover most of what a human driver can do, but not really all that a human driver can do. All of us reach a point of not getting any further. We end-up with self-driving cars that can handle say 95% of the driving task, and there's still that 5% leftover. Upon realizing that we can't get that last 5%, we all agree that AI self-driving cars need to be separated into their own lanes and be treated like a theme park ride, or take other protective measures.

As an overall framework, an AI self-driving car involves these major aspects:
- Sensor Data Collection
- Sensor Fusion
- Virtual World Model
- AI Action Plan Updating
- Car Controls Commands

In terms of sensor data collection, this appears to be a principally physical kind of perception task. It might be likened to the human sensory capabilities. There is though mental processing involved when we humans see things with our eyes and hear sounds with our ears. Thus, mental processing comes to play even in something that otherwise seems like a straightforward peripheral device kind of way. Does a baby come with a brain that has already been pre-wired to best make use of the peripheral devices and also integrate this into the rest of the mental processing of thinking?

For most of the AI self-driving cars to-date, the sensory devices don't do much beyond collecting raw data and at times doing some minimal activities such as compression or transformations. When sensor fusion happens, the data collected from the myriad of sensors needs to be compared to each other and used to create some kind of unified indication about what is going on in the world external to the self-driving car. This is then fed into a virtual world model that is keeping track of where the self-driving car is, where it is trying to go, and other facets. The AI action plans are then updated or devised, and ultimately the AI instructs the self-driving car to take some form of action.

If you take a teenager and try to teach them to drive, do they require thousands upon thousands of driving journeys to figure out how to drive a car? Nope. They can often readily mentally grasp the nature of the driving task, and it becomes more of an effort to coordinate their body to the driving task and less so the mental aspects of the driving task.

The conventional approach to developing an AI self-driving car is to take a blank-slate and try to make it into something that can drive a car. Without an underlying innate capability of the nature that the human brain seems to start with, we might be going at this in the wrong way. We might need to first solve the innate problem, and once that's happened, layering on top to drive a car might be relatively easy and get us to the 100% goal of doing the driving task.

In that manner, perhaps we need to start over and solve the innate capability problem first, and then do the self-driving car aspects. This though would potentially mean that we wouldn't see self-driving cars right away and we might all be discouraged since it would not provide an immediate solution to the problem at hand of wanting to have self-driving cars.

For the moment, we're all kind of locked into making a bridge with twigs, and if it turns out that bridge isn't sturdy enough and won't really do the job, we might need to take another look around and try instead to solve the innate capability problem first. By the way, anyone that cracks the code on the innate capability, they'll likely win a Nobel prize and open the door to AI that we envision we someday all want to see arise.

CHAPTER 7

FREEZING ROBOT PROBLEM AND SELF-DRIVING CARS

CHAPTER 7

FREEZING ROBOT PROBLEM
AND SELF-DRIVING CARS

There were two human chess masters playing a chess game the other day. It was a timed game. Each had no more than five minutes to make their move on the chessboard. After making a move, the player making the move would press down on the top of a small clock-timer on the table to signal that they had made their move. You've probably seen this in various chess tournaments.

At the start of the chess game, they were each slapping the timer as fast as they could get their hands on top of it. The initial moves in a chess game are often lightning fast since the opening maneuvers are all pretty much well studied and practiced. This also tends to happen towards the end game portion of a chess match too, wherein usually there are so few pieces left that the moves are relatively obvious and so the players are quick to make their moves.

Mid-game of a chess match the moves tend to slow down. This is due to being in muddied territory. The chess players opt to study very carefully each move and must contend with the combinatorial explosion involved. By this, I mean that if the player moves a piece to a particular square on the chessboard, they try to think ahead as to the counter move by their opponent, and then their counter move to the counter move, and so on. In chess it is referred to as levels of ply. You

115

can try to think ahead one ply, which is not very hard to do, or try to think ahead a multitude of ply, which can be very mentally taxing.

In this particular chess match that I was watching, the chess players were in deep concentration at the mid-game. Sometimes, the player would reach out as though ready to make a move, and then returned their arm and hand back to their lap or side. Sometimes, the player would put their fingers onto the chess piece, and act as though their fingers were glued to the piece. The player would look at the piece and the surrounding chess squares, and then finally after what seemed like a long time of focus, would then move their piece, and then gently slap the clock-timer. It was obvious that the two players were evenly matched and each was playing at their top form. A battle royale, as it were.

I was transfixed by their play and was watching the chessboard and them at the same time. They would at times lean forward, lean back, brush their hands through their hair, put their hands on the top of their heads as though they would explode, and so on. And then the unthinkable happened. One of the players was seemingly concentrating deeply and apparently lost track of the time (even though there was a timer within inches of their reach). Believe it or not, the time ran out on the player. The player, upon realizing what had just happened, appeared to be crestfallen. He had lost. He tried to argue that it was not a fair loss since he had not actually lost by having been checked or pinned by a checkmate, and nor had he conceded the game to the other player.

The rules were the rules, and he was politely informed that he had lost the chess match. He continued to protest. Do you think he was right that it was "unfair" that he lost the match simply due to running out his clock? Some attendees felt disappointed and wanted to see the two titan players really go at each other and they thought that a mere lack of moving in time seemed untoward to them as a reason to have the match end. Others pointed out that he knew it was timed, and yet he opted to let the time lapse. It was his own fault. Shame on him. No excuses. In fact, if the timer is not really going to be observed as part of the rules, then why even have a timer there at all. Just tell the players they can take as much time as they please. It could become a multi-hours game, or maybe multi-days, multi-weeks, or even multi-decades game.

However you feel about the chess game and timer, one thing is seemingly clear, the chess player froze-up. He had a human freezing problem. This is when you seemingly fail to do something that was otherwise expected to occur, and you "freeze" in place. Maybe you've seen baseball players that freeze-up and fail to swing the bat at a pitch. Or, maybe you've had a moment when you were out hiking and saw a bear, and you froze in position, not sure what to do. It is somewhat common for humans to occasionally freeze when they are expected to take some action or be in motion.

Freezing up can have adverse consequences. We've just seen that the chess player lost the game due to freezing. A baseball player might have taken a strike ball that otherwise could have been hit out of the ballpark. That bear that you saw might come charging at you and had you been nimbler you might have gotten away from its claws. There are some occasions whereby freezing might be good, such as again with the bear and suppose by freezing the bear considered you not a threat or even failed to notice you. But, overall, I think it's fair to say that most of the time a freeze is probably not a good course of action.

People can freeze due to fright. The sight of a bear might be enough to cause your brain to go haywire and you become frozen in fear.

People can freeze due to having their mind go blank. When you see the bear, it might be that you have no prior experience of how to handle seeing a bear, and so your mind has nothing at the ready to tell your body what to do.

People can freeze even though their minds are apparently quite active. In the case of the chess player, he was so absorbed into the chess match that he just lost track of time. Presumably, his mind wasn't blank. Presumably, he wasn't frozen in fear about what move to make. Instead, he was calculating mentally all sorts of moves and counter-moves, and it preoccupied his mind so much that he lost focus on another matter, namely the importance of the timer. He might not have been reflective enough about his own behavior to have caught himself in the act of being totally focused on the chess move.

People can sometimes get confused about time and thus appear to have become frozen. Suppose the chess player thought he had another 30 seconds to go. When the timer went off, it did so sooner than he had expected. He appeared to be frozen, when in fact his mind was calculating the chess moves, and let's say he was counting time too, but misunderstood or was mistaken about the amount of time he was allotted.

Another possibility is that you cannot make up your mind about something and so you intentionally let the clock run out. Suppose the chess player was considering moving the pawn or the queen. He kept going back-and-forth mentally trying to decide which to move. He was so caught up in this internal mental debate that he could not decide. He might have given up at that point and figured he'd just let the clock tick down, or maybe it got to the end of the allotted time and he decided he couldn't make a decision so let fate decide. Of course, in this case, fate was already pre-determined in that the rule was that if you fail to move in time then you have lost the match.

Yet another possibility is becoming overwhelmed mentally and either misjudging time or misunderstanding time. Some chess players have a difficult time concentrating on the chess game and so insist that no one be allowed to cough or sneeze or make any noises during the chess match. Suppose that a chess player is playing chess, meanwhile there are people nearby making noise, meanwhile let's say that the chess player is worried about what he's going to eat for dinner, meanwhile the other chess player is staring at him and so he is trying to stare back. Etc. His mind could be so filled-up with all of this happening that he then forgets about the timer or misjudges it.

For computer people, we might even sometimes say that a person mentally got into an infinite loop. In trying to decide between moving the pawn and the queen, maybe the chess player kept looping mentally over and over. Move the pawn. No, move the queen. No, move the pawn. No, move the queen. On and on this goes. It is similar to a computer program that gets itself caught into a loop that won't stop, notably known as an infinite loop.

What does this have to do with AI self-driving cars?

At the Cybernetic AI Self-Driving Car Institute, we are developing AI software and also caution fellow tech firms and auto makers to make sure that their AI for self-driving cars does not suffer a freeze.

The Freezing Robot Problem

The kind of freeze we are referring to is commonly called the Freezing Robot Problem (FRP).

Imagine that an AI self-driving car is driving down the street. Up ahead is a street sign that kind of looks like a stop sign. It is bent and mauled. You've maybe seen these before — it looks like some hooligan decided to hang on the stop sign and bend it into a pretzel. Now, it could be that it isn't really a stop sign at all, and it just is some kind of art piece that resembles a stop sign. Or, maybe it is indeed a legally valid stop sign and that in spite of the now bent out-of-shape structure it is really truly a stop which must be obeyed.

In this murky aspect of trying to ascertain if the stop sign is true or not, it is possible to encounter the Freezing Robot Problem. Here's how.

Let's assume that the self-driving car is approaching the sign and has ten seconds until it reaches where the sign is posted. We now have a time limit – a decision needs to be made within no later than 10 seconds. If the decision occurs at 15 seconds, it's too late and the self-driving car would likely have already driven past the sign, having merely continued forward since there was no other command from the AI otherwise. If it really is a stop sign, the self-driving car has then broken the law, and possibly endangered other cars and pedestrians.

Some AI self-driving car pundits claim that a self-driving car will never break the law, for which I say hogwash.

Even if the decision can be reached in the ten seconds, let's pretend that for the car to be brought to a halt would require at least 2 seconds. In that sense, making a decision to stop at ten seconds is too late. The real-world time available is only about 8 seconds since there needs to be the time to come to a stop, if that's the right thing to do.

We now have the case of an AI self-driving car which is confronted with trying to determine if there is a stop sign ahead, and the AI has about 8 seconds to do so. There are potential adverse consequences if the AI decides to not stop the car and if the stop sign is truly a stop sign. Of course, you might be thinking, well, just bring the self-driving car to a halt anyway, as a precaution, even if it's not a stop sign, but if you ponder this for a moment I think you'll realize that suddenly coming to a halt can have equally undesirable consequences. The car behind you might ram into you. Etc.

For AI self-driving cars, they tend to have five key stages when processing the world around them and taking action. Those five stages are:
- Sensor Data Collection
- Sensor Fusion
- Virtual World Model Updating
- AI Action Plan Updating
- Car Controls Commands Issuance

The self-driving car that is trying to figure out the situation with the stop sign has to first contend with detecting the stop sign. This would primarily involve the visual sensors such as the cameras on the self-driving car. The images collected by the cameras would be examined by the AI, often using a machine learning model to do so.

This could be an artificial neural network that has been trained on thousands and thousands of images of street signs. The images of this particular suspected street sign would be fed into the neural network. The neural network might indicate that it is or is not a stop sign, or might provide an indication with some amount of probability attached to it. In essence, there's say a 65% chance that it is a stop sign. This though needs to be balanced against the aspect that this implies there's a 35% chance it is not a stop sign.

In theory, the sensor data collection should occur and after having done an assessment in this case of the image, the next stage should take place of the sensor fusion. Let's suppose though that for some reason, the sensor data collection stage won't give up to the sensor fusion stage.

Perhaps the sensor data collection and analysis stage starts to process the image of the stop sign, and the neural network gets bogged down trying to figure out what the image consists of. Meanwhile, the clock is ticking. After let's say 10 seconds occur, the neural network finishes its work and reports that it is a stop sign and then releases into the next stage, the sensor fusion stage. Guess what? It's too late. The AI self-driving car has now proceeded to drive past the sign. Not a good thing.

This is similar to the human freezing problem. The chess player for whatever reason did not finish making his move in the time allotted. In this case, the sensor data collection and analysis did the same thing. It did not finish its efforts in time. This we'll refer to as a Robot Freezing Problem. Bad stuff indeed.

We can reuse the same reasons of why the human freezing problem occurs, and recast it into the Robot Freezing Problem. Essentially, the same conditions that lead to a human freezing can be generally ascribed to the AI freezing. I don't want to overly push the analogy since I want to make clear that today's AI is not the same as the human mind. Today's AI is much cruder, by far. I am just saying that we can use the human freezing problem to inform us about the nature of the Robot Freezing Problem.

First, it could be that the AI is not aware of the time constraint and so it fails to abide by the need to get something done in time. In our view, the AI must be always watching the clock. It must always be estimating how much time is allowed. It must be "self-aware" as to how much time it is using, including even when it is estimating the amount of time that can be used.

Next, the AI can freeze due to becoming too absorbed in a matter at hand. In the case of the stop sign, the sensor data collection and analysis became overly absorbed and used up the available time. The overarching AI system needs to tell each component how much time it can use, and then must monitor the component. When a component goes beyond its allotted time, the overarching AI has to have some contingencies of what to do, especially if the result coming from the component is now empty or only half-baked.

In terms of people freezing when their minds are blank, the analogy to the Freezing Robot Problem would be a circumstance where suppose the neural network receives an image it has never seen before. There is nothing within to help decide what the sign is. In a blank posture, there should be some kind of contingency of what the stage will do. If it reverts to some other more exhaustive means to try and analyze the image, this could be another wrong move since it might use up more time.

For the circumstance of potential confusion leading to freezing up in humans, imagine if the sensor data analysis conveyed to the sensor fusion that the image is muddled and cannot be ascertained. Meanwhile, suppose the sensor fusion is designed in such a manner that if the sensor data analysis is incomplete, the sensor fusion loops back to the sensor data collection stage and tells it to try harder or try again. This could end-up in confusion and the time runs out.

This same example could also be likened to the infinite loop of choosing between the pawn and the queen on the chessboard. The sensor fusion loops to the sensor data analysis. The sensor data analysis pushes to the sensor fusion and offers the same analysis it had done originally. These two get caught in looping back-and-forth with each other. The third stage, the virtual world model updates stage, just keeps waiting for those two other stage to decide what's going on.

The AI system can also become potentially overwhelmed. Suppose besides trying to decide about the stop sign, meanwhile a pedestrian darts out into the street. And, another car that's behind the self-driving car is menacing the self-driving car by getting overly close to it. And, the internal engine sensors are reporting that the engine is overheating. And, one of the computer processors used by the AI has just failed and the AI needs to shift over to a different processor. A lot of things can be happening in real-time simultaneously. This could potentially lead to the AI "freezing up" and not performing some needed action on a timely basis.

There is another possible kind of freeze that could happen with the AI system that is a little bit different than for humans. With most humans, if the human gets frozen, you can usually snap them out of it. I suppose there are circumstances wherein a human goes into a coma, and in that case you might say they have a more definitive and long lasting freeze. Anyway, I'm sure you've had your PC freeze up on you and it won't do anything at all.

Blue Screen of Death Scary for a Self-Driving Car

Imagine that an AI self-driving car system gets itself into a frozen state akin to having the Windows blue screen of death. That's an especially scary proposition for a self-driving car. At least with the other types of Robot Freezing there is a chance that the AI quickly overcomes the freeze, but in the case of a more catastrophic freeze, the question arises as to how soon the AI system can do a reboot or otherwise overcome the freezing.

Furthermore, even if the AI can do some kind of reboot of itself, pretend that the AI self-driving car has been barreling along on the freeway at 70 miles per hour. If the AI system goes "unconscious" for even a few seconds, it can have devastating consequences. This is why the more careful auto makers and tech firms are building into their AI systems a lot of redundancy and resiliency. The act of driving a car is something that has life or death consequences. The AI system needs to be able to work in real-time and deal with whatever bad things might come at it, which also includes the notion that within itself it gets somehow mired or frozen.

The other aspect to consider is that if the Robot Freezing Problem does occur, what provision does the AI have to proceed once it gets out of the frozen mode. It's like when your PC crashes on you and when you bring it up after doing a reboot, Word shows you a recovered document that you were working on. The AI of the self-driving car has to know what the latest status was before the freeze, and rapidly figure out what has happened since then. This kind of catch-up needs to happen in real-time and while at the same time presumably still be properly controlling the car.

One approach involves having a core part of the AI system that is supposedly always on and nearly impossible to have go under. No matter how badly the rest of the AI gets, the core part is intended to still be in action. This could allow the self-driving car to then be slowed down and moved over to the side of the road, or take some other emergency action to try and safely get the self-driving car out of any driving situation that could lead to dire results.

Currently, the efforts involving the AI core are often not extensively tested by the auto maker or tech firm. Right now, the goal is to get the AI self-driving car to perform as a driver of the car. Keep the car in the lanes. Make sure to stop at stop signs. And so on. They pretty much assume that when the AI core is invoked, it will work properly to put the self-driving car into a safer place. It often is not tried in a wide variety of circumstances and just assumed that no matter where the car is when it is invoked, it will work as intended. Until we get more AI self-driving cars on the roadways, and have circumstances of the AI core getting invoked, we might not know how well these AI cores will really function when needed.

Some key principles for good AI self-driving car systems is that they must be continually aware of time. They must be watching the clock and determining whether anything that is running has gone amok or has perhaps overlooked its allotted time or otherwise is not dancing to the needs of the overall operation and safety of the self-driving car. The clock must get top priority. This though also means that the clock watching cannot itself become a problem. Sometimes you can have a racing condition wherein all that happens in a real-time system is getting clock interrupts and as a result actions get delayed or confounded.

There are going to be situations of a no-win nature that the AI system must deal with. There's the famous trolley problem, consisting of having to decide between whether the self-driving car should run into a tree to avoid hitting a child in the street, but hitting the tree might kill the occupants of the car. If the self-driving car does not swerve to hit the tree, it might kill the child standing in the street. The AI components involved in trying to make this kind of ethical decision could take too much time and by default run into the child, or might get into a tussle with each other internally and jam the whole AI system from functioning. This can't be allowed to happen. Presumably. Hopefully.

One other aspect that needs to be considered is the human driver in a self-driving car that's less than a level 5. A level 5 self-driving car does not have a human driver and takes on the driving task, while for self-driving cars at less than a level 5 the self-driving car essentially co-shares the driving with the human, though it is considered that the human driver is ultimately responsible for the self-driving car. Suppose the AI encounters the Robot Freezing Problem – will the human driver even know that it has happened? Will the AI have sufficient core capability to alert the human driver? Will the human driver have enough time available to take over the controls of the self-driving car?

Imagine that you are out camping with a good friend of yours. You are both hiking together in the woods. All of a sudden, your friend freezes up. You don't know why. You can see that he's frozen. But, you don't know why and you don't know how long he will stay in that frozen state. You start looking around, suspecting that maybe a bear is nearby and your friend has seen it. There could though be lots of other reasons why your friend is frozen. As the human driver in an AI self-driving car, you could be in the same circumstance. You don't know why the AI has frozen, and you don't know how long it will last. This is ultimately going to happen and we don't yet know what the end result will be.

Once we have a large volume of self-driving cars on the roadways, ones that are at the less than level 5, we're likely to encounter situations that get the AI into the Robot Freeze Problem. Let's aim to be ready for it, beforehand.

Lance B. Eliot

CHAPTER 8
CANARYING
AND
SELF-DRIVING CARS

Lance B. Eliot

CHAPTER 8

CANARYING AND
SELF-DRIVING CARS

The coal miner looked furtively at the cage holding a canary. There was a chance that in this new part of the mine, there could be seeping carbon monoxide gas. Carbon monoxide is colorless and odorless, and other miners had died by being caught unawares that they were breathing it in. By having the canary, it was hoped that the canary would signal first that there was poisonous gas, and possibly (sadly) even die, but at least the workers in the mine would be able to scuttle out and stay alive and the canary would have saved human lives.

You probably are aware that canaries have been used in mines, as depicted on TV shows and movies that showcase mining as it used to be. Starting around 1911, it was John Scott Haldane, considered the father of oxygen therapy, whom proposed that canaries be used as an early detector of poisonous gases for miners. Miners would often enjoy the sounds of the canary whistling and otherwise be comforted knowing that the canary was there to help the miners to stay alive. Around the 1980's and 1990's, canaries were gradually no longer used and instead automated methods of gas detection were incorporated into mining.

If you are wondering why use canaries rather than say mice, it was Haldane's research that emphasized the anatomical advantages of using a canary as a detector. For flight purposes, the canary has extra air sacs and manages to draw in air when both inhaling and exhaling. This abundance of air sampling and the likely rapid deterioration of the canary in the presence of poisonous gas made these birds nearly ideal for the task. They are also lightweight and relatively small in size, making it easy to carry them into the mines. They didn't require too much care, were relatively inexpensive, and could readily be seen in the semi-darkness of the mines. You can pretty much at a glance know whether the canary is alive or not.

Today, we often use the analogy of having a canary in a cage to suggest that it is important to have an early warning for anytime we might be in a potentially dangerous situation. This doesn't literally mean that you have to use a canary, and instead implies that something should be put in place to act as a detector. The detector will hopefully prevent a calamity or at least forewarn when something untoward might soon occur.

In the computer field, you might already know about the use of so-called canary analysis. This is a technique of trying to reduce the risks associated with moving something from a test environment into a live production environment. We've all had code that we updated and then pushed into production, and then found out that oops there were bugs that hadn't been caught during testing or the new code introduced other conflicts or difficulties into the production environment. In theory, testing should have caught those bugs beforehand and also determined whether the new code is compatible with the production environment. But, the world is not a perfect place and so in spite of what might be even very exhaustive testing and preparations, it is still possible to have problems once an update has gone into live use.

The normal approach to canary analysis consists of opting to parcel out some of your production users (such as say 1% of the users), and they get the changed production system, which becomes the canary part of this, and then a baseline with the same setup, meanwhile the existing production instance remains as is. You then compare the new baseline to the canary, collecting and comparing various performance metrics. If the canary seems to be OK, you can proceed with the full rollout into production. It's like a classic A/B type of testing.

I realize you might debate whether this is truly similar to the notion of the canary in the coal mine. Here, this canary is not going to "die" per se. The canary in this case is presumably going to reveal issues or other facets when comparing the performance benchmarks. I know that you might complain that the canary analogy is only loosely applicable, but hey, it is a vivid imagery of the matter and kind of handy to borrow the canary tale as the concept underlying any early detection mechanism.

There are various automated canary analysis systems in the computer field. Perhaps one of those most notable and popularized would be the Google and Netflix efforts of Kayenta. Kayenta is an open-source automated canary analysis system. The concept is to be able to release software changes at what is considered "high velocity" – meaning that when you want to relatively continuously push stuff into production. This is the agile way of doing systems.

In the olden days, we'd bunch together tons of changes and try to do a big-bang approach to placing into production. Nowadays, it is more of on-the-fly and get new changes into production ASAP. This though also introduces the potential for lots of bad code getting into production, given the pressures to test and get it out the door, and also not knowing how it will really interact with the myriad of other elements of the production system. When I say bad code, it isn't even necessarily that the code itself has bugs or problems, but instead could be that the code introduces some new conflict with other existing aspects of the production system. Thus, the value of using an automated canary analysis to try and detect and prevent unintentional issues emerging in the production environment.

What does this discussion about canaries have to do with AI self-driving cars?

At the Cybernetic AI Self-Driving Car Institute, we are leveraging the canary notion but for a slightly different angle on how it can be applied to technology and AI.

AI self-driving cars are increasingly becoming complex machinery. There are a slew of processors and a large body of AI software that runs on-board the vehicle. For a Level 5 self-driving car, which is the level at which the self-driving car is supposed to be able drive itself and not need any human intervention, the human occupants are totally dependent upon the AI to drive the car. For levels less than 5, even though a human driver is required, and presumably responsible for the self-driving car's actions, the human driver is still quite dependent upon the AI. If the AI falters, it might hand-over the car controls at the worst of times and the human driver might not so readily be able to take corrective action in time.

Every time that you get into a self-driving car, you'll need to ask yourself one question – do you trust the AI of that self-driving car?

Right now, most polls show that people are dubious already about the trustworthiness of AI self-driving cars. Once self-driving cars are prevalent, people will be daily putting their lives into the hands of the AI on-board that car. You might assume that the AI can generally drive the self-driving car, but what about those rare instances involving a situation like being on a mountain road and its nighttime and the road is wet from the rain and a deer suddenly appears in front of the self-driving car? Just because the AI can handle the general aspects of driving does not necessarily guarantee that it can handle more obscure use cases.

Many of the existing AI systems being developed for self-driving cars are tending to focus on trying to catch issues at the time that they arise. That's important, but it also can get the self-driving car into a situation that can be dire or untoward. You'd rather try to catch beforehand if something is amiss or could arise that is amiss.

For airplanes, it is standard practice to do a preflight check. During the preflight check, there is an inspection of the exterior of the airplane to make sure it appears to be air worthy. There is also an interior check. The controls are checked. The wings are checked. Etc. This is sometimes done in a somewhat cursory manner if the plane has been operational and its simply getting ready for continuing on a journey it had already started. In other cases, the preflight check is quite in-depth. This can be due to the plane not having been in use lately, or it can be due to the plane having lots of flying time and periodically you look for subtler cracks and clues of wear. The airlines refer to various levels of checks, ranging from level A to level D.

Our approach is to undertake what we consider an automated "canary" pre-check of the AI self-driving car. It is an added layer of a system that tries to analyze and exercise the AI self-driving car to ensure as best possible that the AI self-driving car is ready for use. Similar to an airline preflight check, the canary can do a full-length and deep analysis, or it can do a lighter partial analysis. The fuller version takes longer to do. The human owner that wants to use the self-driving car can choose which magnitude of pre-check to undertake. We call this added feature PFCC (Pre-Flight Canary Check).

This is essentially a self-diagnostic to try and validate and verify that the AI system and the self-driving car are seemingly ready for travel. I say seemingly because there is only so much that can be pre-checked. Similar to an airplane, in spite of whatever pre-check or pre-flight is undertaken, there is still the chance that once underway that something will emerge that disrupts the journey. There are aspects that might have been able to be found via the pre-check, while there are other aspects that might arise at a later time, during the journey, and no pre-check would have detected.

Let's consider the major stages of an AI self-driving car's actions and how the pre-check takes place. There are these core stages:

- Sensor Data Collection & Analysis
- Sensor Fusion
- Virtual World Model Updating
- AI Action Plans Updating
- Car Control Commands Issuance

First, the PFCC tries to test each of the sensory devices and detect whether they are in working order. Some of the sensory devices have their own built-in self-check, which the PFCC invokes and then determines what the outcome is. Other sensory devices might not have anything already in-place and so the PFCC needs to have specialized components to exercise those sensory devices. In addition to checking device by device, it is also useful to check for multiple devices being used at the same time. A one-at-a-time check might not detect that when more than one at a time are working that a conflict is created or other kinds of issues might arise.

Next, the PFCC tries to check the sensor fusion modules. This involves feeding pre-canned results of data from the sensors as though the self-driving car was already underway. It is a kind of a simulated set of data to see whether the sensor fusion is working properly. Known results are compared to what the sensor fusion currently has to say about the data. There are some non-deterministic aspects that can arise and so checking the latest results to the expected results needs to be done with a certain amount of latitude. It is not necessarily a simplistic pure match comparison.

For the virtual world model, the pre-check is similar to the sensor fusion in that there is a pre-canned virtual world model that is momentarily established, and then updates are pumped to the modules. These modules are responsible for updating the virtual world model. The results are compared to a pre-canned expected set of results.

The AI action plans modules are more challenging to test. They have the greater variability in terms of for any set of inputs what their expected set of outputs will be. So, the PFCC provides a range of canned paths and goals, in order to see whether the AI action plan updates seem to be reasonable. This is a reasonableness form of testing.

In terms of the car controls commands, those are more straightforward for doing the canary check. Based on AI action plan directives, the car controls commands are relatively predictable. This also though requires pre-seeding the modules with the status of the car such that the car controls commands are within the allowed limits expected.

When the PFCC has finished, the question arises as to what to do next. If all is well, as best as can be ascertained, this should be conveyed such that the human owner or occupants knows that the self-driving car and the AI seem ready to proceed. If all is not well, this raises the question of not only notification but also whether the PFCC should indicate that the AI of the self-driving car is so out-of-whack that the self-driving car should not be permitted to proceed at all.

For some minor aspects, the AI of the self-driving car might already have been developed such that it can handle when minor anomalies exist. Thus, the PFCC can feed to the AI that there are now known issues and let the AI proceed accordingly. If the AI itself has issues, the PFCC might need to override the AI system and prevent it from trying to drive when it is not suitable to do so.

The PFCC is something that does not remain static. When the AI of the self-driving car is updated, usually via OTA (Over The Air updates), the PFCC is unlikely to still match to the nature of the AI system and therefore the PFCC will likely need updates too. It also taps into the OTA so that it can be updated as needed to match with the updates of the AI system.

Each type of AI self-driving car, based on brands and models, has its own set of sensory devices, sensor fusion, virtual world model structures, AI action plan structures and processing, and car controls commands. As such, there isn't a universal PFCC per se. Instead, the PFCC needs to be established for that particular brand and model.

One consideration about a pre-flight canary check involves whether it might produce a false negative. Suppose the PFCC reports that the LIDAR is not functioning, but it really is able to function properly. What then? The notion is that it is likely safer to err on the side of caution. The human owner or occupant will be notified and might end-up taking the self-driving car to the repair shop and discover that the PFCC falsely reported an issue. This though is able to be reported and via the OTA will be collected and determined as to whether it requires a global change to the PFCC or other changes are needed.

The more worrisome aspect would be a false positive. Let's suppose the canary could not detect any issues with the forward facing radar, but there really are issues. This is bad. Of course, as stated earlier, the canary cannot guarantee that it will find all anomalies. In any case, during a journey, the AI system is intended to be keeping a log of anomalies discovered during the journey, and this is later on used by the PFCC to try and determine whether there were any issues that arose during the journey that might have been able to be detected earlier on.

Coal miners loved having their canaries. For AI self-driving cars, right now the notion of having a "canary" that can do a pre-flight check is considered an "edge" problem. An edge problem is one that is not at the core of a problem. For the core, most auto makers and tech firms are focused on getting an AI self-driving car to properly drive on the streets, navigate traffic, etc. The use of an extensive and devoted effort of doing a pre-flight check is prudent and ultimately will be valued. Right now, most of the AI self-driving cars on our streets are pampered by the auto maker or tech firm, but we'll eventually have AI self-driving cars being used day-to-day by the everyday consumer. Getting a professional quality pre-flight check is bound to make them as happy as a cheery chirping bird.

CHAPTER 9
NIGHTTIME DRIVING
AND
SELF-DRIVING CARS

CHAPTER 9

NIGHTTIME DRIVING

AND SELF-DRIVING CARS

Are you a nighttime driver? Some people like to drive at night and enjoy pretending they are in their Batmobile and seeking to fight crime. There are some people that reluctantly drive at night -- they drive at night because they need to get home from work or carry out other errands, but otherwise believe that nighttime driving has inherent hazards. There are those that entirely avoid driving at night because they either have difficulty driving at night, or they know that the stats about night driving are scary, or because they believe that vampires come out at night.

Speaking of stats, according to various governmental reports, it is said that there is about 60% less traffic at night but 40% of all fatal car accidents happen at nighttime, furthermore the fatality rate for car occupants is about three times higher at night then during daytime, and the fatal crash rate for 16-year-old drivers is twice what it is at night versus during the day (a good reason to keep your teenager from driving at night!).

What makes nighttime driving so terrible?

One aspect is the impact on visibility. Human drivers depend almost entirely on their vision to undertake the driving task. Without sufficient lighting being available, vision can be impaired. I'm sure you've driven on country roads that had no street lighting, and likely suddenly realized how much light is added to the streets when there are street lamps available. Even when there are street lights, the type of lighting varies, the number of street lights in a given stretch of road varies, and there can be roadway obstructions that block the lighting too. You've got shadows, you've got patches of area that have no direct street lighting, you've got sometimes other bright lights from billboards that maybe add light but can create dancing light and alter colors of lighting, and so on.

I suppose if it was only the lighting that made a difference, perhaps we could all accommodate it as a nighttime issue. But, as you know, there is also driver behavior that comes to play. Drunk driving is much more likely at nighttime than daytime. This means that a driver is likely not able to properly navigate the roads and can either get into an accident or cause someone else to get into an accident. There are also drowsy drivers at nighttime. These drivers are maybe worn out from a long day's work, or maybe they need to get up at 3 a.m. to drive to work in the early morning darkness. Being drowsy causes them to be less aware of the traffic, more likely to swerve or take adverse actions, and be more prone to either getting into an accident or causing one.

I'll punch things up with even more factors about nighttime driving. Since there tends to be less overall traffic at night, it also tends to allow drivers to go faster and perhaps cut corners more so. In addition, I know some drivers that believe they are less likely to get a traffic ticket at nighttime, apparently they believe they are less likely to be caught under the cloak of darkness, so they tell me that they aren't as worried about being full legal in their driving at night. Kind of makes you scared of driving at nighttime with that kind of logic among some drivers.

Oddly enough, it seems like pedestrians and bike riders also become riskier at night. They are already at risk because they cannot be as well seen as they typically can in daylight. You've probably encountered high-risk pedestrians that are willing to jaywalk and dart across the street at nighttime, doing so in front of oncoming headlights, for which those same jaywalkers during the day might not have taken the same chances. Not sure if they do this because they misjudge the cars in the darkness, or whether they somehow believe that the darkness is protecting them from potential harm. Bike riders are also often crazy at nighttime and will either have no lights on their bikes, or if they do they suddenly think that a tiny bike light can generate a beam as bright as the headlights of a car.

What does this have to do with AI self-driving cars?

At the Cybernetic AI Self-Driving Car Institute, we are developing AI for self-driving cars and undertaking special attention to the nighttime driving capabilities.

There are some auto makers and tech firms developing self-driving cars that consider nighttime driving to be nothing more than daytime driving. In other words, they make no special distinction in their AI system as to whether it is daytime driving or nighttime driving. To them, if the AI can handle daytime driving it can ergo handle nighttime driving. Driving is driving, they say.

We respectfully disagree with that somewhat gross over-simplification of the matter. Our viewpoint is that nighttime driving requires added capabilities. That being said, there are some that consider these added nighttime capabilities as though they are a so-called "edge" problem and will concede that yes, there are specialties involved, but it's just an edge matter. An edge problem is one that is not at the core of a problem. Edges are considered something that you get to when you get to it, but otherwise it is not the mainstay of what is needing to be solved. We eschew this notion and instead assert that a good daytime driving AI is not necessarily a good nighttime driving AI. Furthermore, we would even argue that it is unlikely that a good daytime driving AI is a good nighttime driving AI, all other things being equal and if the AI has not been tweaked (as it were) for proper nighttime driving.

In this discussion, let's first establish that there are true AI self-driving cars to be sought, which are considered at a Level 5. The Level 5 self-driving car is one that can be driven without any human intervention needed. The self-driving car is driven by the AI. The AI can drive the car in the same manner that a human can. For self-driving cars less than a Level 5, those such self-driving cars are dependent upon having a human driver in the self-driving car. Indeed, the human driver in those less than a Level 5 self-driving cars is ultimately considered the true driver of the car. In some sense, you could say there is a co-shared driving task responsibility in those self-driving cars less than a Level 5.

For a self-driving car less than a Level 5, it's kind of a ticking time bomb about the issues associated with nighttime driving.

If the AI of the self-driving car has difficulties driving the car, and it occurs at nighttime, there is a danger that if the AI suddenly hands control back to the human driver that's in the car, the human driver might be caught unawares. And, the human driver might have limited visibility due to the darkness, and therefore be impeded in terms of taking corrective action or even being aware of what has caused the AI to toss the football to the human driver. It could be that the nighttime has caused the AI system to become perplexed and so it has handed control back to the human driver, or it could be something not having to do at all with it being nighttime, but for which the human driver is now having to contend with the matter and simultaneously deal with the nighttime aspects too.

For a Level 5 self-driving car, in theory it is assumed that the AI will be able to handle the nighttime aspects of driving. Let's explore ways in which the AI can be impacted by the nighttime driving task, and also how the AI should be enhanced or made to handle the nighttime requirements.

First, perhaps the most obvious aspect is the detriment to visibility. The cameras on the self-driving car will likely not be able to catch as sharp of images and the video will also be less illuminated than were it daytime. The headlights of the self-driving car become particularly vital. If the headlights are in poor shape or occluded due to dust or dirt, it could have an even worsened impact on the image processing. The cameras at the rear of the self-driving car are without any direct lighting such as headlights, and so those are obviously severely degraded in terms of the images captured.

The AI self-driving car should be checking to make sure that the headlights seem to be working sufficiently to capture apt images, as best possible, which can be tested beforehand in terms of doing testing at the start of a journey. The AI can then alert someone, such as a human occupant, and might allow the human occupant to possibly clean-off the headlights or maybe even decide not to start the journey. As a side note, years ago I went to rent a car, drove the rental car off the lot during daytime, and then when it reached nighttime I turned on the headlights – found out to my shock and surprise that the headlamps were burnt out. If I had checked during the daytime, I likely would have switched to another car, or only used the car during daylight, or taken some other action. Keep this in mind the next time you rent a car!

The image processing of nighttime images is different than the image processing for daytime images. Images that are well lit can be more readily processed. Images that have dark shadows and other darkened portions is harder to process. This often involves doing various image processing clean-up. It can also change the probabilities associated with object detection. An object that during daytime had say a 100% probability of being a wheelchair at the curb might at nighttime have a 60% chance of being a wheelchair.

There is also typically much more light reflections and distortions. Street light and the headlights can bounce off the car ahead of you, perhaps doing so off the chrome bumper that acts like a kind of mirror, and thus other objects either become more well-lit or become overly lit. The bouncing light can actually cause a sunburst effect and make the object recognition harder. Again, the image processing software has to be ready for this impact.

For machine learning and the use of artificial neural networks, if those neural networks were trained with pictures of those objects during the daytime, it could be that those objects are no longer detected by the neural network. It's important the training of the neural network include objects as seen in darker conditions. Some prefer to do both daytime image and nighttime image training together, as a smorgasbord, while others believe that the neural network will be better off if one instance is trained to daytime images and the other to nighttime images.

One aspect that visually can become more problematic is the detection and interpretation of street signs. During daylight, it is usually relatively easy to spot a street sign, such as a stop sign or a caution sign. At nighttime, it can be much harder to spot the street sign. The darkness might obscure it, or the brightness of the headlights might create a sunburst effect. As mentioned, if a machine learning approach was used to train on street sign detection, it is important to be mindful of whether it can handle nighttime versions.

Many self-driving cars use various relatively simple road-following techniques when the AI is driving the car. For example, the roadway markings are examined and used to decide where the boundaries of a lane are. Some roads use flat paint to mark the lanes, while some use reflective Botts' dots. Nighttime driving can be tricky in trying to figure out where the lane markings are. It can also be easy to be fooled by the road markings in terms of falsely believing that they are correct when in fact they might be something left over from prior markings that have since been changed. The AI system portions dealing with this need to be prepared for nighttime driving.

So far, I've focused mainly on the sensory aspects of nighttime driving. Consider that there are five key stages involved in AI self-driving cars during the driving task:

- Sensors Data collection and interpretation
- Sensor Fusion
- Virtual World Model updating
- AI Action Plan preparation
- Car Controls Command issuance

During sensor fusion, the sensor results are compared and combined in various ways. If the cameras are not getting good images, it is usually the case that the AI system is devised to give less weight to those sensors. Thus, if the camera is suggesting that there doesn't seem to be a pedestrian at the side of the road (perhaps the image is so darkened that there is no ready way to detect a figure standing in the shadows), but the radar is detecting that something might be there, the sensor fusion has to determine what to do. Should it rely upon the radar and claim that there is a pedestrian there? During daylight, often times the sensor fusion opts to wait until the cameras are able to agree with the radar results. This though can be dicey depending upon how much time is available before a decision about the matter needs to be made.

Overall, at nighttime, the cameras are likely be much less reliable and thus the sensor fusion should be designed to cope with this aspect. It's almost the same as a human driver. If a human driver cannot readily see at night, they are at heightened risk of properly performing the driving task. Purists for AI self-driving cars point out that the aspect of multiple sensory devices on an AI self-driving car presumably implies that therefore the AI self-driving car will be better able to do nighttime driving than a human can (most humans don't have radar or LIDAR built into their bodies). This is a somewhat arguable point in that yes the self-driving car has other sensory devices that a human does not have, but it then belies the aspect that humans are (for now) generally better at the "intelligence" aspects of driving than the AI systems of this era are so far.

The virtual world model that is used by the AI must also be updated and be apprised of the nighttime aspects. This can include that the associated probabilities with detected objects are going to be lower than the normal daytime driving, as mentioned about whether a wheelchair is at the curb or not. And, the AI action plans need to take into account the now somewhat degraded virtual world model, along with what kinds of actions can be taken in nighttime situations.

Suppose the AI decides that a hard braking action is needed. At nighttime, the driver behind you might not be as ready to stop, versus during daytime they might have more readily been aware of you ahead of them. Too, keep in mind that the human drivers on the roads at nighttime are potentially drunken or drowsy, or cannot see the road and the traffic as well as they could during daytime. The AI needs to consider how other drivers will be acting and reacting at nighttime. This might also dictate that the AI needs to be going slower or taking other defensive maneuvers that would not necessarily be needed during daylight hours or used as frequently.

I'm sure that some proponents for AI self-driving cars will instantly say that there shouldn't be any human drivers on the roads, and that we need to get to the point of having only AI self-driving cars out there. Thus, there would be no need for the AI to worry about human drivers at nighttime. No more drunken human drivers that leave the bar after midnight and then crash into other cars. No more drowsy human drivers that wake-up before sunrise and are so sleepy when they drive that they ram into a pedestrian.

Instead, nighttime driving will be a breeze. The AI self-driving car would communicate via V2V (vehicle to vehicle communications) with other self-driving cars, and they would all help each other in nighttime driving conditions. The AI self-driving car ahead of you might have figured out that there's a pedestrian standing at the crosswalk, which perhaps your AI self-driving car cannot quite determine due to the darkness and angle, and shared this aspect with your AI of your self-driving car. Cross sharing would aid the AI's in doing enhanced nighttime driving on a collective and collaborative basis.

Sure, this might well happen, but it's going to be far off in the future. There are about 200 million conventional cars in the United States today. Those are not going to magically become AI self-driving cars right away. For many decades to come, we will have a mix of human driven cars and AI self-driving cars. You cannot be designing AI self-driving cars for only the day in which we have exclusively AI self-driving cars, since we are putting AI self-driving cars on our streets today. The streets today and for the foreseeable future will have human driven cars. That's a fact.

This brings up another aspect about AI self-driving cars that is worthy of important consideration about nighttime driving. There are predictions that we will likely be using AI self-driving cars on a round-the-clock basis. And, it makes sense to do so. You have a car that will go wherever you want it to, with a built-in driver that doesn't need to rest. If you own an AI self-driving car, you are likely to turn it into a revenue generating ridesharing vehicle. Most AI self-driving cars will probably be driving around on a 24x7 basis.

How does this tie into nighttime driving? It means that as AI self-driving cars become more popular and prevalent, there will be more and more of them on our roadways at nighttime. This means a higher likelihood of getting entangled with a drunken human driver or a drowsy human driver. It would seem a reasonable bet that the first rash of AI self-driving car accidents will most likely arise at nighttime, once AI self-driving cars become prevalent.

What might hopefully aid in offsetting the encounters with human drunk drivers will be that those humans that were going to drive drunk will instead use a ride sharing service, of which, maybe there will be an abundance due to the prevalence of AI self-driving cars. This does though bring up the aspect that some ask me about at conferences, namely, how will an AI self-driving car handle a drunken occupant?

If you have a human driver for say Uber or Lyft, the human driver sometimes will talk with the human drunken passenger or even physically aid them to get into and out of the vehicle. The AI is not going to be able to do the same, for now. I've mentioned that most AI self-driving cars will be outfitted with cameras pointing into the car, and audio capabilities, such that the human owner of the AI self-driving car can at least see and talk with the human occupants.

There are more twists and turns about nighttime driving for AI self-driving cars. Imagine that it is nighttime and there are heavy rains coming down. When you combine the weather with the nighttime aspects, it can be a potent danger for any driver, human or AI.

Another twist is roadwork. Generally, most of the roadwork that we have done on our infrastructure is done at nighttime, which is done to reduce the adverse impact to daytime traffic. For the AI to contend with roadwork can be difficult, and especially so at nighttime. Trying to figure out that the street is coned off and you can't make a right turn up ahead, it's not easy to do at nighttime.

As they say, do not go gentle into that good night, but instead rage, rage against the dying of the light. We need to have AI systems for self-driving cars that realize there is a difference between daylight driving and nighttime driving. Treating daylight as the same as nighttime, or assuming that nighttime driving is equivalent to daytime, it's a dangerous trap that could cause a grave and overbearing darkness to descend upon the future of AI self-driving cars.

CHAPTER 10
ZOMBIE-CARS TAXES
AND
SELF-DRIVING CARS

CHAPTER 10

ZOMBIE-CARS TAXES AND SELF-DRIVING CARS

Quill gets overturned by the unassuming but blockbuster court case of South Dakota versus Wayfair Inc. What's that about, you might ask? The United States Supreme Court ruled that online retailers will now be required to collect sales taxes in states for which those online firms have no actual physical presence, assuming that the respective state wants those retailers to collect such taxes (duh, yes, most states if not all will – its "free" revenue for the state!). Brick-and-mortar firms cheered feverishly and popped champagne when they heard the ruling. Online retailers cursed out loud and were dreading this possible decision.

Here's the skinny.

At the start of the 1990's, the Supreme Court had ruled in the Quill Corporation versus North Dakota case that online retailers could not be forced to pay sales taxes in states for which they did not have a substantial connection in. Pretty much if the online retailer had no physical offices or warehouses in a state, it was nearly impossible for the state to try and hit them with sales taxes.

For online retailers, this was a godsend.

First, it meant that their goods could be sold without having to include the added cost of sales tax in the state for which an item was ordered by a customer. Physical stores were maddened at this decision since it meant that they were inherently more expensive than if you bought something online. You might counter-argue that the online retailer has to charge you shipping, while the local store does not, but the cost of shipping has come down dramatically, plus many consumers don't think about the true cost of ordering online (they often neglect to add the shipping cost when they compare in-store prices versus online prices).

Second, online retailers, while laughing all the way to the bank, claimed that it was just too byzantine to try and collect the sales tax for every state. They argued that the effort to calculate the sales tax for this state and for that state, would be an undue burden. It would jack up their costs unfairly. A physical store in state X only has to collect sales tax for items sold as based on the sales tax of state X. Meanwhile, the online retailer would have to figure out the sales tax for state A, B, C, D, and so on. It would be a nightmare.

Online retailers have had a free ride, one might say, since the early 1990s. The ride is over. Now, they will need to collect the sales tax for any item they sell that is purchased by a customer in whatever state the customer is in. Will this be horribly complex? Most would say that with the advent of modern day computers, trying to calculate the sales tax is no longer a manual or laborious burden and it doesn't really matter how many states you are selling into. It's a few lines of extra code in a program. So, that prior argument about added complexity is now out the window.

Will states decide they want to hit online retailers with a sales tax. Of course, since it is "free" money. Imagine how much additional revenue a state can take in. It's a windfall. Plus, the brick-and-mortar firms in a state will argue, as they have all along, the states "must" charge the online retailers with a sales tax as a matter of fairness and logic. The logic part is that why would a physical store want to be in a given state if the state is going to let the online retailers get away without paying sales tax. It puts the physical store at a disadvantage. Meanwhile, the physical store likely is helping the state economy in many other ways, including hiring people in that state, perhaps making use of local vendors in that state, and otherwise helping that state to be vibrant.

Justice Anthony Kennedy indicated in the written opinion by the majority in the 5-to-4 ruling that states have been losing out on about $33 billion in annual sales tax revenue. Ouch! States are now already starting to figure out how they will divvy up all that sales tax revenue that will be pouring in. A lot of special interests in each state will want to grab a piece of that pie.

One important aspect that with hindsight we can perhaps concede is that the lack of a state-by-state sales tax might have aided the advent of the online retailers. Perhaps, if there had been a sales tax imposed, there might not be as many online retailers today, or the big ones might not be as big. As a society, by allowing online retailers to be unburdened by the sales tax, we might have allowed the innovation of online retailing to grab hold. It is like a new plant that we carefully protected from the other fauna, so that it could take root. Now, the new plant is presumably established enough that it can exist without special exemptions. That's the hope or thought about why we did not force the online retailers into collecting state sales taxes for their online sales.

Do you think that online retailers will now be curbed or substantially harmed because of the Supreme Court ruling? It's admittedly hard to see that it would. The trend towards online purchasing has hammered the brick-and-mortar world. Physical stores and malls have been devastated. It would appear to be an unstoppable trend. Seems unlikely that just because the online retailers now will be charging you sales tax that you'll say to yourself, darn it, I'll go over to my local mall and buy that item there instead.

What does this have to do with AI self-driving cars?

At the Cybernetic AI Self-Driving Car Institute, we are developing AI systems for self-driving cars, and also identifying key trends of where self-driving cars and AI is headed. It seems likely that we'll soon enough see states opting to impose so-called Zombie-cars usage taxes.

Zombie-cars?

Yes, some like to refer to self-driving cars as zombie-cars. Kind of cute, I suppose. For those of you AI developers that are pouring your hearts into making true Level 5 self-driving cars, which are self-driving cars that can drive without any human intervention and are supposed to be able to drive as a human could, it would seem somewhat disheartening to think that some would call your creation a zombie. Zombies are brain dead. At least call the self-driving car a Frankenstein, which though considered a monster, it did have something of a brain.

Zombie-cars usage taxes?

Yes, there will likely be usage taxes imposed onto zombie-cars. Well, another way to phrase things is that there are going to be "self-driving car" usage taxes, which if OK with you is how I will refer to it henceforth herein. Just don't like the connotations about those zombies.

Let's consider what will happen once AI self-driving cars become prevalent. Most are predicting that self-driving cars will be working non-stop. You have a built-in chauffeur that never sleeps and is always available to drive the car. When you are at work, no sense in having your AI self-driving car sitting out in the parking lot. Put it to use! Especially if you can make money by doing so. The odds are that most people that own a self-driving car are going to turn it into a ridesharing revenue source. Running it essentially 24x7, you can recoup the costs of the self-driving car (hopefully) and maybe make a profit besides.

Where is your non-stop AI self-driving car going to go? If you live in city Y, you'll most likely want to keep your self-driving car relatively close in case you need it, so you'll rideshare it for people in city Y that need to get a lift. Suppose that there are hundreds, maybe thousands of these AI self-driving cars, all cruising around your city. It would be akin to an Uber driver that is cruising around, waiting for a request for a pick-up.

You probably won't have the self-driving car be parked, and instead keep it moving. You'll likely even be using some kind of Big Data analytics system that will help predict where your self-driving car should be. If it's nearing 2 a.m. and the bars are closing, seems like that's the part of town where your ridesharing AI self-driving car ought to be.

Anyway, imagine these self-driving cars crisscrossing city Y. Seems like it will impact the roads there in city Y. Today, during late hours, those roads are hardly used. In the future, there might be roads that are getting non-stop usage. Non-stop usage of the roads means they'll wear out more. Roads that wear out more need greater amount of upkeep and repairs. Greater upkeep and repairs costs money. Where will the money come from for those rising costs? Answer: AI self-driving cars.

You can expect that local cities, the states, and the federal government will allow wake-up and realize that the popularity of AI self-driving cars has caused a tremendous strain on the roadway infrastructure. If the cause of the problem is due to AI self-driving cars, perhaps make that cause also be the solution. Impose a usage fee on AI self-driving cars. The money raised would presumably go towards the infrastructure that supports those roving beasts.

Of course, there are some governmental entities that might opt to use the money for some other purpose entirely. They might decide that spending the money on homelessness or other local societal aspects is preferred over spending it on infrastructure. The infrastructure angle is usually the way to get society to buy into the usage fee, since it suggests a tit-for-tat. If the AI self-driving cars caused added costs for infrastructure, they should pay for it. That would seem fair to most, though maybe not necessarily to the owners of the AI self-driving cars. On the other hand, once a government finds a spigot that pours out money, they'll likely spend it as they wish.

This brings up an important point that ties back to the online retailers and the sales taxes by state. Remember that it was viewed as a crucial breathing space for online retailers to grow and prosper by not having had a sales tax burden to meet. Would the imposition of a usage fee possibly curb or disrupt the advent of AI self-driving cars? If so, do we want to cause an innovation that appears to have great societal payoffs get "harmed" by having to deal with usage fees? This is going to likely require a significant amount of open public debate.

You might wonder how the owners of AI self-driving cars could possibly complain about a usage fee, since if indeed their vehicles are impacting the roadways it seems befitting that they pay for it, somehow. Their counter-argument would be that the AI self-driving car is providing other societal good. For example, by providing a ready mode of transportation, these cruising non-stop self-driving cars are offering a form of "public transportation" and that perhaps a municipality is able to cut-back on their costs for busses and other forms of mass transit. It would be unfair to hit the AI self-driving cars with usage fees and neglect the fact that these vehicles are already doing so much for the city or locale.

The debate about the appropriateness of a usage fee is going to likely bounce back-and-forth. Meanwhile, let's consider how usage fees would even be ascertained. The usage fee should presumably be based on one or more usage factors.

Here's some of the most likely usage factors:
- Per occupant
- Per delivery
- Per miles driven
- Per time driven
- Per trip

One means would be to require the AI self-driving car to self-report the number of occupants in the car, for any trip that takes place. There could be a usage fee charged per occupant. The owner of the AI self-driving car would need to decide whether to pass along the cost to the occupants, or absorb the usage fee otherwise into the cost of doing business. This approach though seems perhaps intrusive in that it requires counting people. Furthermore, if you have one person that goes one hundred miles, while there are five people that go two miles, it doesn't seem sensible that if the cost is a fixed fee per occupant that the shorter trip has the higher usage fee.

There's another drawback of using occupants as a factor, namely that if the AI self-driving car is used to delivery pizza, and there's not a human occupant needed, the AI self-driving car would travel around the city without having to pay any usage fee. Thus, another factor would be to impose a per delivery fee. This would be eagerly done by many cities that want to catch revenue for the Amazon deliveries, and for the food GrubHub deliveries, and the like.

We can combine these factors. Perhaps there is one level of a usage fee for the occupant's model, and a different level of a usage fee for the delivery model.

Another approach says that rather than caring about what the AI self-driving car is doing, charge a usage fee for the number of miles driven. This would be handy too since the occupant or delivery models assume that the self-driving car is being used for a particular purpose. If the AI self-driving car is cruising around, and there's no occupants and no delivery underway, perhaps because it is staying in motion to most likely be near to wherever it is needed when so needed, the miles driven approach would make sure that the usage fee applies.

You can argue that the miles driven metric has its own advantage and disadvantages, and so you could possibly end-up suggesting that maybe the better approach is based on time. Time takes distance out of the equation. If the AI self-driving car is on the roadways, and moving at one mile per hour for five hours, maybe that's more important than if it was being driven for 80 miles per hour for thirty minutes. You could also try to argue in favor of using the number of trips as the usage metric, but that's squishy since who's to say exactly what constitutes a trip.

We can mix-and-match these metrics. We can also add various conditions. Maybe the usage fee is based on the metric of time during the morning hours, and then it shifts into the metric of the number of miles driven, doing so for the afternoons and evenings. You might at first complain that having varied limitations and metrics is going to be onerous to calculate, but that's kind of the same argument used in the early days of the online retailers. With today's vastly superior computing power, I don't think you can make much of a case about things being labor intensive to calculate.

Notice that I mentioned that the AI self-driving car would self-report its usage. How would it do this? It could keep track of the miles driven, or the time underway, or the number of occupants, and so on. This tracking could then be communicated to a municipality via the OTA (Over The Air) updating capability that AI self-driving cars are going to have. It would seem relatively straightforward that the AI self-driving car would be required to report its numbers say each day, or each week, and the government would then receive those numbers and charge the usage fee.

You could even consider using blockchain to have the AI self-driving cars record their usage, and then have the government tap into the blockchain to impose the usage fees.

I'm sure there will be cheaters. There are bound to be AI self-driving car owners that will try and find a means to avoid the usage fees. Since the numbers are presumably self-reported by the AI self-driving car, there could be a method to hack your AI self-driving car so it under-reports the numbers. It is likely the government would need to try and audit the AI self-driving cars and determine if there is anything funny going on about the reporting aspects.

The government could also potentially use other means to try and verify the self-reported numbers. With the advent of V2I (vehicle to infrastructure) communications, the roadway infrastructure is going to be able to track our cars in ways not as feasible today. It is conceivable that the infrastructure will know exactly where your self-driving car has been the entire day and can calculate the usage fee without even asking your AI self-driving car for the numbers.

All this potential collecting of data about the AI self-driving car raises potential privacy issues. We'll have to see how that plays out in the usage fee debates.

One final point to consider. We had the tension between the brick-and-mortar stores and the online retailers. The emergence of AI self-driving cars as ridesharing vehicles is certainly going to create tension with human-based ridesharing services. This includes taxis and shuttles, but also includes those everyday folks that are trying to make some money by being a rideshare driver. What will happen to them? Maybe the usage fee of AI self-driving cars will help save them, since it might make the costs of using an AI self-driving car higher than choosing the human-driven approach.

Or, maybe to be "fair" we'll have usage fees on any ridesharing service, regardless of AI based or human-based. As you can see, there are lots of public related considerations that go into all of this. The revenue though of Zombie-cars is just going to be so tempting that no one will be able to overlook it. You can bet that there will be many start and stop attempts to come up with usage fees on those Zombies. The zombie apocalypse will need to pay for itself.

CHAPTER 11

TRAFFIC LIGHTS

AND

SELF-DRIVING CARS

CHAPTER 11

TRAFFIC LIGHTS
AND SELF-DRIVING CARS

There are maybe 300,000 of these in the United States alone. You see them every day. You notice them, but you don't notice them. They save lives, but are generally unheralded for what they do. Sometimes you curse them. Sometimes you thank them. Can you guess what I am referring to?

Answer: Traffic lights.

Yes, as human drivers you are surrounded by traffic lights. Most major intersections have them. You watch for that green light so that you can zoom through the intersection. When you see the yellow light, you need to judge whether to hit the brakes before the light turns red, or maybe hit the accelerator to try and make it before the light turns red. It's a game.

It's actually a deadly game. There are an estimated 700 deaths per year due to red-light running crashes. That's sad and preventable. Equally horrific, there are an estimated 126,000 injuries due to red-light running. That's sad and preventable. The next time you see some nut rush through a red light, I hope you'll realize the crazy danger involved and perhaps adjust your own driving to no longer try to rush through a traffic signal.

When you think about it for a moment, you'll realize that traffic signals are kind of a scary mechanism since they don't do anything to actually physically stop anyone from driving crazily. It is all a voluntary

163

system. It is our collective belief in the traffic signal that makes it real. The traffic signal does not toss down a huge net to stop cars that disobey the light. It does not spring forth spikes from the roadway to stop cars that are going to potentially ram into another car. Instead, it is just some lights that we as humans have generally agreed to abide by.

Imagine though the chaos without the traffic signals. We would either all be having continual near misses, or the intersections would need to have stop signs or some other control mechanism, which would likely stall traffic and make our driving times longer. You could put traffic officers at intersections, which is the way things used to be, prior to the advent of traffic signals. A traffic officer would stand in the intersection and direct traffic. At one point, New York City had something like 6,000 traffic officers to direct traffic. The traffic signal put a lot of those traffic officers out of the job of directing traffic, though they were still needed for various other traffic related duties.

When traffic signals first began, they were often a signboard that said the word Go and the word Stop. The Go signboard would pop-up, and after a bit would be pushed down. The Stop word would pop-up and then after a bit be pushed down. Human operators at first stood nearby and controlled these signboards. Eventually, it was quasi-automated. Traffic signals were at first only with two lights, one that said Go and one that said Stop, or had the red light and the green light similarly. Ultimately it became clear that human drivers would not judge things well when there were only two modes, and thus a third light was born, a yellow light, which helped to reduce the frequency of intersection crashes. The yellow light became a handy warning to drivers that the red light would be coming soon.

Since the red light is perhaps the most important of the three lights (I don't want to get into a debate about that here, but I think you generally agree that the red light is quite important!), it is normally placed at the top of the three lights that are on a traffic signal. Next is the yellow light, at the middle, and logically in sequence of what then comes next, namely the green light at the bottom. Not all countries do things this way. But, it is pretty common and makes sense that you would want them at least to have the traffic signal in a Red-Yellow-

Green or a Green-Yellow-Red sequence. A Yellow-Red-Green or a Yellow-Green-Red would seem counterintuitive and likely confusing, even if we all agreed to it.

How long does each color light get lit? I realize that if you've ever sat at traffic signal for what seemed like an inordinately long time, you might claim that the red light seems to be at times glowing for an hour or more. Well, the reality is that many traffic signals are established with pre-timed intervals but usually for a duration of just some set number of seconds (not hours). The green goes for X number of seconds, the yellow goes for Y number of seconds, and the red goes for Z number of seconds. This is the easiest way to "program" a traffic signal. What should the values of X, Y, and Z be?

For yellow lights, there is a rule-of-thumb that many use. The rule-of-thumb is that the yellow light should be set for 1 second for each 10 miles per hour of the posted speed nearby. Thus, if the posted speed is 40 miles per hour, the yellow light should last for 4 seconds. It doesn't have to be set for that interval of time, and some locations use something like 3 seconds to maybe 6 seconds for all of their yellow lights (rather than having to figure out per each intersection what the nearby posted speed is).

The setting of the time for the green light and for the red light is trickier. If you arbitrarily pick a number of seconds, it could be that it hampers traffic. A street leading into the intersection that has a lot of traffic should presumably have a longer green light, so as to allow more traffic to get through the intersection. Sometimes you get to a traffic signal that is "dumb" and it seems to allow the same amount of time for both the red light and the green light in each direction, but this bottles up the roads leading in that have a lot of traffic, while it infuriates those drivers too when the light is green for the mildly traveled road that has no traffic streaming through the intersection.

Traffic engineers will sometimes study traffic patterns and then advise that a traffic signal should be setup in somewhat savvier timings. This can help with the flow of traffic through the intersection. The problem here though is that for most "dumb" traffic signals they can only set one value for X, one value for Y, and one value for Z. This then means that regardless of the time of day, it is going to stay with the same interval times. This explains why at midnight you sometimes sit at an intersection when there is no other traffic around. It has a pre-timed setting that does not vary.

At some intersections, they put pressure plates in the street to try and detect car traffic. The pressure plate is activated by the weight of the car, and the plate then informs the signal that a car is waiting. Rather than a pressure plate, it can be a magnetic detecting plate that is activated by the metal in your car. In any case, the point is that the traffic signal is coordinated with something that tries to detect traffic. For the plates, it is mainly that a car is sitting still and waiting. The plates aren't usually tracking traffic per se.

In the early days of traffic signals, the traffic signal would ring a bell to indicate when the light was either changing colors or when it was red. Today, very few traffic signals make any such sounds. We are all inside our car cocoons and it would seem unlikely that having a sound would help us particularly, and it would be a likely irritant to those that live or work near the traffic signal.

What does this have to do with AI self-driving cars?

At the Cybernetic AI Self-Driving Car Institute, we are developing AI software for self-driving cars and consider the traffic signal aspects as a crucial capability for self-driving cars.

Some auto makers and tech firms consider the advanced traffic signal problem to be an "edge" problem in that it is not core per se of the act of driving a car. Allow me to qualify that point. Certainly we all agree that being able to detect a traffic signal is at the core of the driving task. But, this can be done in a rather simplistic manner, or it can be done in a more advanced manner. For some, once the simplistic version has been figured out, they move on to other self-driving car capabilities and consider the traffic signal problem entirely solved.

Let's take a deeper dive into the topic of traffic signals.

First, how do you know that a traffic signal exists?

I am sure you are thinking that my question seems kind of silly and the answer is obvious. You look out your windshield and you see the traffic signal. Duh. Well, as humans, we have an incredible ability of our eyeballs and our ability to see. We can look at a scene and find the gorilla that's hidden over there behind the stack of boxes. Similarly, we can look at the street scene up ahead and "know" where the traffic signal is.

The sensors on the AI self-driving car have to put in a bit more work. The cameras capture images of what's ahead of the self-driving car. The image needs to be analyzed by the system. The image might contain not only a traffic signal, but perhaps there's a plane flying through the sky that can be seen behind the traffic signal, maybe there's a few birds resting on the traffic signal, maybe there's rain coming down and the traffic signal is partially obscured by the heavy rain. And so on.

It's not such an easy thing to find the traffic signal in a picture. Yes, the traffic signal is likely the same kind of shape nearly all of the time. It's usually on a post of some kind. It's got the three lights. It's hanging over the intersection. These are all valuable clues. I'm not saying it is rocket science per se to find the traffic signal, but it is more work than you think.

So, the first step involves capturing images via the sensors and analyzing those images to find the traffic signal. You want to find the traffic signal and also not be fooled by something that might resemble a traffic signal. There could be other nearby lights such as for a lit-up billboard or maybe lights on the exterior of a building. Those might be red lights, yellow lights, green lights, and so you cannot just look for a particular color of a light.

You also might be faced with a circumstance of an intersection that does not have a traffic light. If the image analysis says that it cannot find a traffic signal, does this mean for sure that there isn't one there? Maybe yes, maybe no. It could be that the image analyzer capability could not find the traffic signal. If the sensor analysis reports to the sensor fusion that there isn't a traffic signal, and if turns out there is one there, the result could be catastrophic.

Let's consider the stages of the AI self-driving car processing:
- Sensor data collection and analysis
- Sensor fusion
- Virtual world model updating
- AI action plan preparation
- Car commands control issuance

Let's pretend then that the visual sensor and analysis did not find a traffic signal, but that the traffic signal does exist. The sensor feeds its results into the sensor fusion. The sensor fusion compares each of the sensory device indications to try and triangulate and make sure that no one sensor is misleading or maybe has failed to do its job.

Would the radar on-board of the AI self-driving car detect the traffic signal? This can be tricky in that the radar might not have enough of a profile to bounce the radar signal off the traffic signal and detect it. Would the LIDAR detect it? This depends on whether there is even LIDAR available (for Tesla's they aren't using LIDAR). Anyway the point is that a traffic signal could exist but not be detected by any of the sensors of the AI self-driving car.

Imagine then that the self-driving car believes that it can just barrel through the intersection. This could be wrong to do and perhaps there is a red light and the cross traffic is going through the intersection. Crash!

Now I realize you might object and say that the AI self-driving car has hopefully detected the other cars that are going through the intersection and so would realize that something is afoot. Furthermore, if there is other traffic next to the AI self-driving car, it would presumably be slowing down and stopping, due to the presumed red light, and so the AI self-driving car should notice that the other cars nearby it are stopping and so it should consider stopping too.

This brings up my earlier point about simplistic traffic signal capabilities versus more advanced traffic signal detection capabilities. If the AI and the self-driving car is solely programmed to visually find the traffic signal, this can be a significant risk as to being able to properly determine when a traffic signal is present or not. Some AI systems for self-driving cars only do the visual detection. Adding the sensor fusion and the other sensors data is considered "more advanced" – and likewise, comparing to the traffic situation is even more advanced. In other words, if you are only thinking of the traffic signal as just an object, you would only care whether you detected that particular object or not.

We know though as humans that we use all sorts of other clues to figure things out. I'll add more twists to the traffic signal problem. Suppose the traffic signal is there but it is not working? Maybe the power is out, maybe it has had a failure, etc. I know you might think that it low odds that a traffic signal exists but is not working – it is though a possibility.

It is a very real possibility that you might not even be able to see a traffic signal such as suppose you are driving behind a big truck as you come up to an intersection. Your view is blocked by the truck. The AI of the self-driving car has to be advanced enough to deal with these various scenarios. Keep in mind that this is all life-or-death stuff. A wrong move by the AI self-driving car can harm the human occupants of the AI self-driving car, and harm other humans by hitting other cars or maybe hitting a pedestrian, etc.

Another variant to deal with involves the visibility of seeing the traffic signal. Suppose the camera has dirt on the lenses and only gets a partial image. The lighting nearby the traffic signal can also impact detecting the status of the traffic signal. Have you ever driven up to an intersection and the sun was directly in your eyes? You barely could see the traffic signal lights. You knew that there was a traffic signal there, but it was nearly impossible to see if the light was red, yellow or green.

Indeed, you've undoubtedly noticed that most modern traffic signals make use of hoods to help protect the light and make the light stand-out. Often, a traffic signal light is aimed at a particular angle to try and make it more visibly apparent. These elements can help the image processing. They can also make the image processing more difficult, depending upon how much the hood hides the light or that angle of the light is a kilter of where the camera on the car is.

One hope is that the future traffic signals will be "smart" instead of dumb. The smart traffic signal has more advanced capabilities than the traditional "dumb" one does. For example, a smart traffic signal might emit an electronic signal indicating the status of the traffic light. In that case, the AI self-driving car can potentially receive an electronic signal rather than relying only on a beam of light. This can significantly aid the detection of the traffic signal.

Those that are looking further into the future would even say that the traffic signal as we know it today will ultimately no longer exist. If we later on opt to get rid of all human driven cars, and we had only AI self-driving cars, presumably the use of lights to signal the status of the traffic signal is no longer needed. It could be just an electronic signal. Also, there would not be a need to have the large pole that currently houses the traffic signal. You could put the traffic signal electronic emitter in a squat box near to the intersection instead.

I like to point out to those futurists that it will be a long time before we have only AI self-driving cars. For the foreseeable future, we will have a mix of human driven cars and AI self-driving cars (there are around 200 million conventional cars today in the United States alone). As such, we'll need to keep the light emitting traffic signals for those "darned" human drivers. There are experiments currently involving sending an electronic signal to your smartphone, thus, in theory, we might be able to have human drivers that rely upon their smartphones to let them know the intersection status, rather than looking at a traffic light. I don't think that's going to hold-up though and we are likely to continue with the traffic signals as they are.

Where we will likely have advances towards smart traffic signals will be the ability of the traffic signal to adjust the timing of the lights based on more informed traffic analytics. A city might have traffic detecting sensors throughout the city, some being on buildings, some embedded in the roadway, some collected via flying drones, and so on. These sensors will collect traffic info. The traffic info will be analyzed and fed to the traffic signals so that the traffic signals can adjust their timing. This could greatly reduce gridlock.

Your AI self-driving car might also get connected to these traffic analytics. Perhaps your AI self-driving car realizes that the traffic for the next six blocks is slowed due to the traffic signals at the intersections straight ahead. It might be able to predict that if the self-driving car makes a right turn up ahead and then goes onto another street, the self-driving car can avoid the bottlenecks up ahead. The AI could either opt to take the alternative route, or speak to the human occupant and ask permission first whether the alternative path is OK with them.

There will be the advent of V2I (vehicle to infrastructure) for AI self-driving cars. This means that AI self-driving cars will be able to electronically communicate with the street infrastructure, including the traffic signals, and with bridges (which can indicate how crowded they are), and tolls, etc. All of that will aid in navigating traffic signals. There is also going to be V2V (vehicle to vehicle communications), involving self-driving cars electronically communicating with other self-driving cars. This will be handy akin to my earlier example of cars around you that are coming to a stop at an intersection – not only would the AI self-driving car presumably directly detect this, but the other self-driving cars might be sharing with your AI self-driving car that they have detected that the intersection up ahead has a broken traffic signal so they are all coming to a stop.

Smart traffic signals might have some unintended consequences. Suppose a hacker was able to connect to a traffic signal and force it to show whatever red/yellow/green the hacker wanted to display. Suppose the traffic signals are all interconnected so as to allow for timed activity across the entire city, but then the hacker can opt to control all of those at once. There is also the privacy aspects that maybe a traffic signal is observing traffic and capturing license plates or other info about the cars passing through the intersection – would this be a good thing or a bad thing? It might help when trying to find criminals, but it might be used for nefarious violations of privacy.

Here's one that might be somewhat chilling too. Should your AI self-driving car be allowed to run a red light or not? You might argue that the AI should never be allowed to carry out an illegal act. But, suppose that you are bleeding to death as a human occupant in an AI self-driving car and there are no other cars nearby, wouldn't it be OK to run the red light so as to get to a hospital? There are numerous scenarios involving situations of these kinds. Also, if your AI self-driving car does run a red light, should it tell the police? Should it issue you a ticket?

There's a famous joke about traffic signals and green/red lights. Here's a short version of it. Let's pretend you get into a ridesharing car by Uber or Lyft and the human driver heads to your destination. At an intersection that is a red light, the driver goes through the red light without stopping. You are startled by this. You ask the driver why didn't he stop at the red light? He says that his brother never stops at red lights and it works well for him. While you are thinking about this, another red light nears and he drives through that one too. Catching your breath, all of sudden as the driver approaches a green light he jams on the brakes. What, you ask, why in the world did he stop at a green light? He turns to you and says, because I thought my brother might be coming along through the intersection from the other road.

Funny? Maybe. But with AI self-driving cars we need to make sure they are well versed in dealing with traffic signals. The simplistic approach might be OK for the moment, when we have only a few AI self-driving cars on the roadways, and while they are used only in carefully mapped and geo-fenced areas. Once AI self-driving cars become more prevalent, it will be a life or death matter as to whether they can handle traffic signals. This means that the AI needs to become more advanced. I'm giving a green light for that to happen.

CHAPTER 12
REVERSE ENGINEERING
AND
SELF-DRIVING CARS

CHAPTER 12

REVERSE ENGINEERING AND SELF-DRIVING CARS

At an annual auto show there was a Tesla Model 3 chassis shown on the convention floor, being displayed by a company other than Tesla. Notice that I said it was just the chassis, and not the entire car. You might be wondering why would somebody be showing off a Tesla Model 3 chassis? Did they lose the rest of the car? Or, did they somehow surgically remove the chassis from the rest of the car? It might seem odd that they weren't showing the entire car.

Answer: Reverse engineering.

It is a well-known secret in the auto industry that the auto makers are desirous of knowing every tiny detail about their competitor's cars. To find out the details usually involves taking apart an entire car, piece by piece, bolt by bolt. Some of the auto makers have their own inside teams that will buy a competitor's car and take it apart. Other auto makers will pay an outside company to do the same. There are companies that specialize in doing reverse engineering on cars. They delight in buying the latest model of any car, and meticulously taking it apart like so many Lego blocks.

More than being a delight, these reverse engineering firms can make some good bucks by their efforts. They will sell to other auto makers what they find out about their competitor's cars. You get a full documented list of every item that went into the car, along with useful added aspects like how much each component likely costs. Furthermore, they can estimate how much it cost to assemble the parts and give another auto maker insight into what kind of assembly effort their competition is using.

An auto maker will even at times pay to get the same insights about their own cars! I know it seems odd, since you would assume that an auto maker would already know how they assemble their own cars and what it costs, but it can be very handy to see the estimates made by the third party. The third party might be high or low, or otherwise not so exacting. It is also handy to know what they are telling your competitors. Plus, you can then have them do a comparison for you to the parts and costs associated with your competitors versus your cars.

The company at the auto show was touting the aspect that they had taken apart the Tesla Model 3 and could tell you whatever you wanted to know about the car. They can tell you the weight of each part. They can tell you the size of each part. They can tell you the cost. They call tell you how capable the part is. They can tell you where the part was made as in the U.S or overseas. In many cases they can even tell you what the composition of the part is, such as percentages of metal versus other elements.

To give you a sense of the magnitude of this cataloging of a car, a rule-of-thumb is that a typical everyday car might have 50,000 or more parts, and it might require something like 200,000 distinct manufacturing steps. Just image that if you were designing a new car, it would be handy to learn from the other cars on the marketplace. Maybe try to use the carburetors that are found on a Brand X Model Y and the mufflers that are on a Brand Z Model Q. If you are an auto maker, you might also discover that you are overpaying for your own carburetor and realize that to reduce costs and ultimately reduce the price that you charge for your car that you ought to switch.

There's an added twist to this reverse engineering effort. In theory, if you are careful as you take apart a car, you can also scan the parts into a CAD system and essentially reverse engineering the entire design of the car. With today's powerful CAD systems, you can then view the car from any angle and dive into and zoom in and out of the whole design of the car.

Some really sophisticated CAD systems will allow you to pump the design into a simulator program. This could allow you to potentially act as though the car exists and see how it runs. In a video game kind of way, you can possibly "drive" the car and see how it handles. You can simulate what the gas mileage will be like and examine other facets of the car.

What does all of this have to do with AI self-driving cars?

At the Cybernetic AI Self-Driving Car Institute, we are developing AI systems for self-driving cars. You might find of keen interest that the same industry wide pursuit of reverse engineering of conventional cars is now underway for AI self-driving cars too.

Let's consider first the physical elements of an AI self-driving car.

There are five key stages to the processing aspects of an AI self-driving car:

- Sensor data collection and interpretation
- Sensor fusion
- Virtual world model updating
- AI action plan updating
- Car commands controls issuance

The most prominent physical aspects of an AI self-driving car are the sensors. There are a multitude of sensors on an AI self-driving car, including radar sensors, sonic sensors, cameras, LIDAR, IMU's, and other sensors.

Each auto maker and tech firm is keenly interested in knowing which sensors the other companies are using in their AI self-driving cars. It's a somewhat free-for-all right now in that there is no dominant supplier per se. Indeed, the various companies that make sensors suitable for AI self-driving cars are in a fierce fight over trying to gain traction for their sensors.

This makes a lot of sense when you realize that today there are 200 million conventional cars in the United States alone – so assume that those will ultimately become obsolete and be replaced with an equal number or greater of AI self-driving cars. You'd want your sensors to be the first-choice for those hundreds of millions of new cars. Plus, you would guess that anyone that grabs the United States market will be very likely to become the global supplier too. Big markets, big bucks to be had.

Not only is it useful to know which sensors are being used, but it is also valuable to know where they are placed within the AI self-driving car. The design of a self-driving car is still being figured out. How can you best embed these sensors in the car? You want the sensors to be free of obstruction. You also want them to be less vulnerable to the elements. At the same time, they have to look stylishly placed.

The early versions of LIDAR were large and looked like some strange beanie cap on the top of the car. It stood out. Some thought it looked cool, but most thought it looked kind of dorky. The LIDAR devices are getting smaller in size, better in performance, and coming down in cost. This allows for placing it in a manner that it does not seem so visually awkward. It still though needs to be able to freely emit the light beams and so it cannot be buried inside some other aspect of the car.

So, knowing what sensors your competitor is using and how they are placing them into or onto the body of the self-driving car is important insider information. If your competitor does a better job then you, it might cause consumers or businesses to want to buy their AI self-driving car rather than your AI self-driving car. It might seem shallow to AI developers to think that someone will choose an AI self-driving car by how it looks, versus by what it does in terms of the AI capabilities, but I assure you that the average buyer is going to be focused more on looks than what the self-driving car AI can actually achieve, all else being seemingly equal.

In addition to the sensors, you would also want to know what kinds of microprocessors are being used. Once again, there is a battle royale going on in this realm. Imagine that an AI self-driving car might end-up with dozens upon dozens of microprocessors, maybe in the hundreds. Multiply that number by the 200 million cars in the United States in terms of ultimately replacing those cars with AI self-driving cars. It's going to be a huge bonanza for the chip makers.

Indeed, there are chip makers that are now producing and striving to further advance specialized chips for AI self-driving cars. They hope to get into the early AI self-driving cars and become the defacto standard. It's like the early days of Beta versus VHS. Which will prevail? If you can get rooted into the marketplace, it will be hard to upset your placement. That's why you see these latest artificial neural network chips. They are going to be needed aplenty on AI self-driving cars.

Where should these microprocessors be placed inside the body of the car? For some of the early day self-driving cars, they pretty much went into the trunk. The trunk was sacrificed to be jam packed with the computers used by the self-driving car and the AI. If your competitor has slickly found a means to put the microprocessors in the underbody, while you have used up the trunk, and their self-driving car has a fully available trunk, which self-driving car do you think will get chosen by consumers and businesses? Again, doing some reverse engineering could let you know whether you are ahead of the game or behind the game.

You might also discover during your reverse engineering that your competitor has made "mistakes" or at least gotten themselves into some bad spots. Suppose your competitor put the microprocessors in an area of the self-driving car that is subject to heat. This could suggest that after their self-driving cars are on the roads for a few weeks or months that those chips will start to burn out. The competitor might not realize it now and only discover this month from now. Should you tell them? Well, normally you wouldn't want to give advice to your competitors that makes them better off.

This does though bring up an ethics question. If during your reverse engineering of a competitors AI self-driving car that you find something untoward that could lead to the harm of humans, should you inform the competitor? You might say that you have no such obligation. It's up to your competitor to find out and deal with it when it occurs. But, if you don't warn them and it harms human occupants or others, are you in a sense culpable? Maybe it would be good to let the competitor know. Or, if you prefer, inform the marketplace and it will cast your competitor in a bad light, which presumably would be good for you.

There is a next level of detail in terms of reverse engineering an AI self-driving car. We focused so far on the physical aspects that are relatively easy to discern. You can take apart a car and readily identify the sensors and the chips, etc. What you cannot so readily reverse engineer is the software.

Each auto maker and tech firm making AI self-driving cars is eager to know what the software is and does in their competitors self-driving car. Sure, some of it might be open source, but most of it is more likely to be proprietary. Indeed, the auto makers and tech firms are protecting their software as though it is gold that belongs in Fort Knox. Who can blame them? The arms race is on. Everyone is trying to figure out how to make the AI be as truly AI as possible.

The AI software is going to ultimately be what makes or breaks a true AI self-driving car. For a level 5 self-driving car, which is the level that involves the AI fully driving the car and there is no human driver needed, we are all trying to get to that nirvana. It's not going to be easy. There have been millions upon millions of dollars spent on software engineers and others trying to develop this AI code. Firms would want to protect it from prying eyes.

Once the AI code is loaded into the self-driving car, it's possible to try and reverse engineer it. I know that some of you are saying that this doesn't seem possible to do, since the code is presumably compiled or otherwise being interpreted and the auto maker or tech firm certainly didn't load the source code into the on-board computers. You are right that the source code would not be on-board. But, you are wrong if you think that the running software cannot be reverse engineered.

There are plenty of available reverse engineering software tools in the marketplace. If you can get to the memory of the chips, you have a shot at reverse engineering the code. Especially if some of it is open source. I say this because you can already know what the target of the open source is, and thus those portions of the running code can be more readily discerned. This then gets you into the right spots to look for the proprietary stuff.

The artificial neural networks and the machine learning portions are even easier to figure out, usually. If you know the key models used for neural networks, you can somewhat readily find those patterns in the memory and drives of the on-board systems. You can then reverse engineer it back into the overall models with the number of neurons, the weights, and all the rest.

What would make this even more doable would be if you were an AI developer already developing such systems. You would already be aware of the nature of the coding needed for these kinds of systems. If you took an everyday Python or C++ coder they would be highly unlikely to be able to figure this out. It requires software engineers with more detailed and machine-based experience and skills. This narrows the pool of potential reverse engineers, but doesn't drop it to zero by any means.

That being said, it is important to emphasize that the auto makers and tech firms need to make sure they are sufficiently protecting their AI self-driving car systems from these kinds of reverse engineering efforts. Besides protecting the Intellectual Property (IP), it also needs to be done to try and prevent hackers from doing nefarious things. Having hackers that can break into and figure out how the AI systems are working is something nobody wants to have happen. To-date, the AI self-driving car field has been less careful about the security aspects than they should be. The focus has been on making an AI self-driving car. That's good, but not good enough in the sense that having an AI self-driving car vulnerable to security breaches is a very bad thing.

You might be wondering whether this reverse engineering of cars is even legal. Can you really take apart a competitor's car? Generally, yes, once you've bought the car, there's nothing that legally stops you from physically taking it apart per se. If you try to copy their car parts or car design, you might then find yourself in violation of their IP. If you merely are studying it, that's something hard to outlaw.

In the case of reverse engineering the software, that's something that does tend to run afoul of the law. You might know or remember the Digital Millennium Copyright Act (DCMA) that was passed by the United States Congress in 1998. The DMCA was pretty much a push by the entertainment industry that was worried about protecting unauthorized copying and dissemination of their copyrighted works. Firms put in place Technical Protection Mechanisms (TPM's) to prevent hackers or others from doing reverse engineering. Circumvention of a TPM is considered a form of reverse engineering. This is considered generally illegal throughout the United States and has been adopted by much of the rest of the world as being considered illegal too.

There are narrow exceptions for law enforcement purposes, or for national security purposes, and for selective computer security research purposes, but otherwise it's against the law to circumvent a TPM in order to reverse engineer software. There have been attempts to make the case that bypassing TPM's for certain kinds of systems should be purposely allowed, doing so for the good of society. Suppose an AI self-driving car has some hidden bugs, or vulnerabilities, or other malfunctions – wouldn't you and society benefit by allowing "experts" to delve into the software and figure out how it works and identify those perhaps death-producing problems?

If you are thinking about doing a teardown of your own AI self-driving car, I'd advise against it. The odds are that you'll end-up with thousands of parts and have no idea what they do and why they are there. Also, if you are thinking you might put Humpty Dumpty back together again, I assure you that the odds of putting back together a torn apart car is most likely futile. It's not just a Rubik's cube that you need to move the positions back into their proper places. In any case, we're definitely already seeing some amount of reverse engineering of AI self-driving cars and it will continue and gain momentum as self-driving cars become more prevalent.

You could say it's a Darwinian kind of thing in that the industry will find what works and what doesn't work, and perhaps more quickly get toward what does work, having done so by involuntarily by having their cars reverse engineered. Excuse me, I've got to get back to taking the bolts out of that AI self-driving car I bought last week.

Lance B. Eliot

CHAPTER 13

SINGULARITY AI

AND SELF-DRIVING CARS

CHAPTER 13

SINGULARITY AI
AND SELF-DRIVING CARS

AI of today is considered narrow, brittle, and not at all near to what any of us might reasonably agree is a true sense of intelligence. Today's AI is exciting and helping to advance the role and capabilities of computers, but do not mistake this advancement with becoming sentient. Being able to beat top chess masters or Go players with today's computing capabilities is not a sign of true overall computer-based intelligence. With faster processors and machine learning and lots of data, we still don't have our finger on what it means to achieve agency. In a sense, we are still on the path of computational empowerment – and the grand question is whether somehow someway someday that with maybe a startling breakthrough we might tip over into true intelligence. It's the essential tipping point.

Are you the person that's is going to have some flash of insight that gets us across the chasm between contemporary narrow AI and over into AGI (Artificial General Intelligence)?

I hope so! I'm pulling for you to be the one. AGI is the nirvana that most AI researchers are aiming to reach. AGI would be a system that can exhibit the kind of intelligence that you see even in a young child, combining aspects of common sense reasoning with overall reasoning and with whatever else we want to ascribe to intelligent behavior. I would say that those of us slaving away at AI for all so many years are hoping that others will come along and jump on our shoulders and get us to the next step in AI evolution.

There are some that believe you'd be better off forgetting what has already been done in AI, and start with a blank sheet. Maybe the ways we've devised so far are really a dead-end. You might try mightily to get to the next step, and it won't ever happen because you are mired in what was done in the past. Thus, some say that you should shove aside the AI of today and think anew. I say if that will get us to AGI, go for it. Seems a bit over-the-top and I would think that even if what has been done today, even if the wrong path, we could learn from it and go toward another direction, but anyway, if it's too much of an anchor than I am with you to drop it cold.

Suppose we get to AGI, then what happens?

Some would say that we would have true AI. We would presumably have robots that actually can do the intelligent things that people do. It's an open debate whether robots could physically do what humans do at that juncture. In other words, maybe we aren't yet able to perfect the physical mechanisms of robots and so we have otherwise been able to imbue them with mental intelligence but not yet physically built them to be like humans. Some believe that there is a tie between us humans in terms of our bodies and our mental processes, such that a robot won't be able to be as intelligent as a human unless it has a "body" akin to a human body. Others eschew this connection and say that you can have any kind of robot you want, having no body per se or some other kind of "body" and that it just won't matter – the intelligence is a different beast altogether.

So, let's say for the moment we do reach AGI, and it maybe it is in a robot or maybe not, since we aren't sure whether the body aspects matter for reaching AGI. Does anything come after AGI, or is AGI the final end-point of artificial intelligence?

Artificial Superintelligence, a Step Beyond AGI

Well, some would say that there might be a step beyond AGI, namely ASI (Artificial Superintelligence). ASI would be the exceeding of human intelligence. AGI arrives at what we consider everyday intelligence, while ASI takes us beyond Einstein and beyond any kind of human intelligence we've ever known. We're not even sure what this ASI would consist of. That makes sense, though, because we are trapped by our own human intelligence. Maybe our human intelligence lacks the imagination that would enable us to envision what superintelligence consists of.

Let's just say that the ASI is like merging together all intelligence of everyone and it combines and synergizes. All rolled into one. And that whatever embodies this superintelligence will have that kind of mental capability. Does this mean that ASI includes an ability to read minds and have telepathy? That seems like a kind of cheating in that it goes beyond what seems like intelligence as we know it, but, hey, maybe you do get to read minds once you go beyond AGI. Who knows?

Take a look at Figure 1.

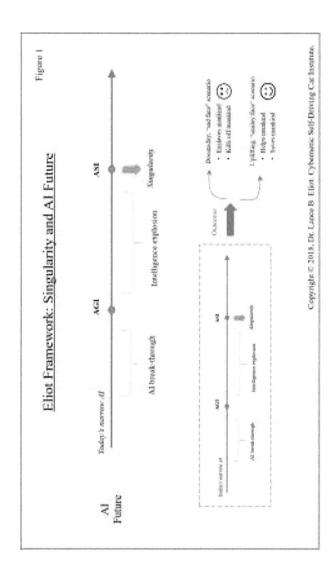

There is AI as we know it today, and which ultimately hopefully we'll get to AGI, though maybe it requires us taking some kind of alternative path that we don't even know about today. It could be that AGI is the end all. There might not be anything beyond AGI. Maybe we'd all be happy to have computers that have the same mental capabilities as us. But, it could also be that there's something beyond us, and the AGI might become ASI.

How would the AGI become ASI?

If humans got today's AI to become AGI, maybe we can push on AGI and get it to evolve into ASI. Or, maybe we aren't smart enough to do that. Maybe the AGI will somehow be smart enough, even though it presumably is only just as smart as us. On the other hand, maybe the AGI when running on computers all around the globe all the time can figure things out that us humans cannot.

And so there are some that believe the AGI will encounter an intelligence explosion, as it were, and fuel upon itself to become ASI. There will be a kind of runaway reaction of self-improvement by the AGI. Think of this like a nuclear reactor that goes "critical" and there is an incredible mental chain reaction. Some would say that this could happen and be entirely out of human hands. We presumably don't start it, other than we were the ones that got us to the AGI stage, and we nor can't stop it once it gets underway. There aren't any nuclear rods to pull out to slow down or stop the reactive matter.

I know that there are plenty of science fiction movies that depict this kind of thing. In some plots, the humans are unable to prevent or stop this from happening. In other cases, they manage to pull the plug just in time, or maybe take hammers and bats to the computers to disrupt them during the chain reaction. Or, a clever human happens to have a USB stick containing a computer virus that they manage to plug into their home PC and it infects the ASI everywhere, halting it in its tracks. By the way, so that you can sleep at night, rest assured I keep such a USB stick next to my bed at night, just in case.

Well, maybe.

ASI Emerges to Singularity

Anyway, this act of ASI emerging is often referred to as singularity.

Will we reach a point of singularity? It's hard to say. It would seem like we need to first get to AGI. For those of you that are overly ambitious, you might say that you are going to skip AGI and go directly to ASI and get us to singularity. Good luck on that.

Let's assume that singularity happens, then what? Is there something that comes after ASI? So far, it seems like most predictions are that either ASI opts to enslave all humans and/or kills off mankind, or, ASI embraces humans and helps save mankind and extends mankind. It seems like most people are thinking that the singularity will perceive us humans as nothing more than bugs or cockroaches, and so a vote today would probably produce the doomsday or "sad face" scenario as considered most likely. If its Ok with you, I'll side with the glass is half-full group, and I'll vote that the singularity likes us and has intelligence that can see the better side of things, so this is the "smiley face" or uplifting scenario.

With man's inhumanity to man, I realize it maybe seems hard to believe that the singularity will consider us worthy. But, hey, maybe it will give the singularity something fun and challenging to do – it will seek to shape up mankind, and do so without actually enslaving us. That's a pretty good mental problem to try and solve, you must admit. Wouldn't a superintelligence want and maybe even need tough problems to solve?

Take a look next at Figure 2.

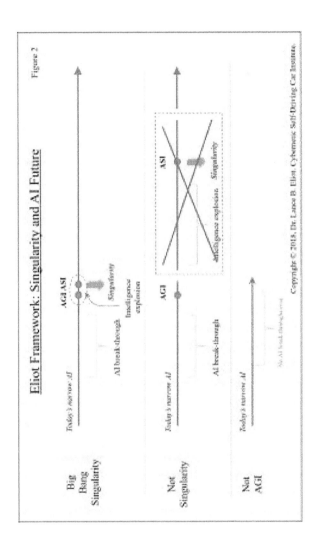

Eliot Framework: Singularity and AI Future   Figure 2

Copyright © 2018, Dr. Lance B. Eliot, Cybernetic Self-Driving Car Institute.

Will there be any substantial time between the achieving of AGI and the reaching of ASI? It could be that the intelligence explosion takes maybe weeks or months, maybe even years. It might sneak up on us. Or, it might slowly occur, and we know it is happening, and maybe we don't mind since the ASI looks pretty good along the way. Are we lulling ourselves into then getting smacked when the actual singularity happens? You pick the outcome, smiley face or sad face.

There are some that suggest the AGI achievement will instantaneously produce the intelligence explosion and we'll have ASI in some nanoseconds or picoseconds. Bam, we got AGI but then we got ASI, all in the blink of an eye. If you are the sad face outcome person, this is a bad thing and the crossing of the bridge on AGI was not where we should have gone. If you are the smiley face outcome person, this is a good thing and we didn't need to wait around to achieve ASI. Singularity happened and we didn't even see how it occurred, it just did.

That's the Big Bang Singularity.

You could argue that there won't ever be a singularity. Instead, we'll reach AGI and that's it. There is no more there. The AGI will be like us. Maybe it can make more of us, and we can make more of it. But, we can't get the AGI to become ASI, and nor can the AGI get itself to become ASI. We've reached the pinnacle of intelligence, regardless of human based or computer based in form and capability. I know this seems kind of disappointing, since we are always wanting to reach to the stars and find new conquests. But, hey, if you are the sad face outcome person then you are relieved to think that the AGI is it. No worries about the possibly nefarious singularity.

I'm not sure we'll be able to put together a proof that singularity cannot ever occur. In that sense, there will still be an urging and ongoing conquest ahead. I envision teams of AGI and humans, working arm in arm, trying in vain to find the vaunted ASI. It could go on forever.

That's the Not Singularity. Maybe we can refer to it as waiting for Godot.

Let's now consider whether we can reach AGI. I believe in my heart we can, but admittedly there's not much right now that seems to argue for it. As mentioned before, the AI of today is only so qualified. If you put more processors into it, will that spark it to intelligence? If you have massive amounts of computer memory, will that do it? Even if we go quantum computing, is that really the spark or just the same kind of algorithms and computations that we are using today to do our narrow AI. It might make narrow AI really good, but will it bump us up to AGI?

There's the Not AGI.

I'll refer to it as the false hope. We might have a false hope that we can dramatically shift today's AI into becoming AGI. For those of you that believe the Big Bang Singularity, it's a relief to believe in the Not AGI, if you also believe that there's a sad face outcome after reaching singularity. Much of this anguish has been expressed in other ways, and perhaps the famous book and movie about Frankenstein covers some of this ground.

What does all of this have to do with AI self-driving cars?

At the Cybernetic AI Self-Driving Car Institute, we are developing AI for self-driving cars. We assert that there won't be true AI self-driving cars until we all master at least common sense reasoning for AI, and perhaps also only if we also reach AGI.

I know those are fighting words. Allow me to explain.

There are various levels of self-driving cars. At the level 5, it is considered a true self-driving car, one that is driven by the AI and that no human driver is needed. The AI can drive the car as a human can and does not require human assistance. Self-driving cars at less than a level 5 require a human driver. This means that the human and the AI co-share the driving task. This though has inherent problems and can create potential and deadly results.

Some believe that the path to a Level 5 self-driving car is by first achieving a Level 4, or maybe even a Level 3 and jumping up to a Level 5. Others believe that you can skip the lower levels and aim to directly reach a Level 5. In whichever way we get there, the question is whether or not with the AI we know today that we can reach a true Level 5 self-driving car.

You might have heard on the news that we seem to already have true Level 5 self-driving cars. I assert that's a debatable claim. If you have a so-called Level 5 AI self-driving car that needs to be geo-fenced and that requires to already have detailed mapping of its surroundings, and if when it encounters an "abnormal" driving situation it must revert to only stopping the car and pulling to the side of the road, well, I don't know about you but that's not the Level 5 that I'm aiming for as a true Level 5 self-driving car.

Some say you don't need common sense reasoning to be able to drive a car. I'm not so sure that's a valid claim. Some say that the driving task is a very narrow task, like say playing chess or playing the game Go. I'm not so sure that's a valid claim. It seems to me that if we are wanting to have a self-driving car that can be driven like a human driver, it requires that the AI be able to exhibit the same kind of intelligent behavior that a human driver does.

It is my postulation that we need more AI than we have today, and it is a kind of AI approaching the AGI that is needed, in order to fulfill a goal of having a true Level 5 self-driving car. Without those kinds of advances, I'd say we'll be mired in a "5-ish" level self-driving car, but for which we would all reasonably agree is not a true Level 5. This doesn't mean that the 5-ish level self-driving car won't be useful, it certainly can be. We can get a lot of mileage out of it (sorry about the pun!), it just won't be the same as a human driven car.

Now, if you are the sad face outcome person, you might say that we should be satisfied if we can get to the 5-ish level self-driving car, because maybe if we push to AGI in order to get to a true Level 5 self-driving car, we end-up with the AGI that bursts into ASI and all of mankind is destroyed. That's a rather haunting viewpoint and might deter some AI developers, but probably not many. I'd say that most AI developers are wanting to either reach AGI, or reach a true Level 5 self-driving car, or both.

Indeed, you could see it as:

- It could be that our efforts to achieve a true Level 5 self-driving car will be the driving force that gets us to AGI.

- Or, it could be that we will otherwise discover AGI and then apply it to the area of AI self-driving cars and thus achieve the true AI self-driving car.

If we all somehow breakthrough to singularity, what happens with AI self-driving cars?

The sad face scenario is that the singularity takes over all of our AI self-driving cars and uses it in one fell swoop to try and kill us all off. In that sense, we have provided a mechanism for our own self-destruction by building and fielding the AI self-driving cars, just to make things easier for the ASI that decides we've got to go. Oops.

I'd prefer to end the discussion by focusing on the smiley face scenario.

The singularity, if it occurs, realizes that we need our AI self-driving cars, and improves it in ways that we couldn't possibly achieve. These become Level 6 self-driving cars, or maybe Level 10 or Level 100. The singularity or ASI opts to benefit all of mankind and AI self-driving cars is just one of many ways in which it opts to do so. That's the ASI that I'm hoping for.

Here's then my final vote on all this. Hold onto your hats.

We will indeed collectively achieve AGI and it will be an essential aspect for also achieving true Level 5 self-driving cars. There won't be the Big Bang Singularity and instead it will occur over a somewhat lengthy period of time. During that singularity emergence, we'll become at peace with the ASI and the world will be a better place for it.

If that's too much smiley face for you, sorry about that, but I'm a glass is half-full kind of person. Or, am I just saying this because I am worried about Roko's Basilisk.

APPENDIX

APPENDIX A
TEACHING WITH THIS MATERIAL

The material in this book can be readily used either as a supplemental to other content for a class, or it can also be used as a core set of textbook material for a specialized class. Classes where this material is most likely used include any classes at the college or university level that want to augment the class by offering thought provoking and educational essays about AI and self-driving cars.

In particular, here are some aspects for class use:

o <u>Computer Science</u>. Studying AI, autonomous vehicles, etc.

o <u>Business</u>. Exploring technology and it adoption for business.

o <u>Sociology</u>. Sociological views on the adoption and advancement of technology.

Specialized classes at the undergraduate and graduate level can also make use of this material.

For each chapter, consider whether you think the chapter provides material relevant to your course topic. There is plenty of opportunity to get the students thinking about the topic and force them to decide whether they agree or disagree with the points offered and positions taken. I would also encourage you to have the students do additional research beyond the chapter material presented (I provide next some suggested assignments they can do).

RESEARCH ASSIGNMENTS ON THESE TOPICS

Your students can find background material on these topics, doing so in various business and technical publications. I list below the top ranked AI related journals. For business publications, I would suggest the usual culprits such as the Harvard Business Review, Forbes, Fortune, WSJ, and the like.

Here are some suggestions of homework or projects that you could assign to students:

a) Assignment for foundational AI research topic: Research and prepare a paper and a presentation on a specific aspect of Deep AI, Machine Learning, ANN, etc. The paper should cite at least 3 reputable sources. Compare and contrast to what has been stated in this book.

b) Assignment for the Self-Driving Car topic: Research and prepare a paper and Self-Driving Cars. Cite at least 3 reputable sources and analyze the characterizations. Compare and contrast to what has been stated in this book.

c) Assignment for a Business topic: Research and prepare a paper and a presentation on businesses and advanced technology. What is hot, and what is not? Cite at least 3 reputable sources. Compare and contrast to the depictions in this book.

d) Assignment to do a Startup: Have the students prepare a paper about how they might startup a business in this realm. They must submit a sound Business Plan for the startup. They could also be asked to present their Business Plan and so should also have a presentation deck to coincide with it.

You can certainly adjust the aforementioned assignments to fit to your particular needs and the class structure. You'll notice that I ask for 3 reputable cited sources for the paper writing based assignments. I usually steer students toward "reputable" publications, since otherwise they will cite some oddball source that has no credentials other than that they happened to write something and post it onto the Internet. You can define "reputable" in whatever way you prefer, for example some faculty think Wikipedia is not reputable while others believe it is reputable and allow students to cite it.

The reason that I usually ask for at least 3 citations is that if the student only does one or two citations they usually settle on whatever they happened to find the fastest. By requiring three citations, it usually seems to force them to look around, explore, and end-up probably finding five or more, and then whittling it down to 3 that they will actually use.

I have not specified the length of their papers, and leave that to you to tell the students what you prefer. For each of those assignments, you could end-up with a short one to two pager, or you could do a dissertation length paper. Base the length on whatever best fits for your class, and the credit amount of the assignment within the context of the other grading metrics you'll be using for the class.

I mention in the assignments that they are to do a paper and prepare a presentation. I usually try to get students to present their work. This is a good practice for what they will do in the business world. Most of the time, they will be required to prepare an analysis and present it. If you don't have the class time or inclination to have the students present, then you can of course cut out the aspect of them putting together a presentation.

If you want to point students toward highly ranked journals in AI, here's a list of the top journals as reported by *various citation counts sources* (this list changes year to year):

- o Communications of the ACM
- o Artificial Intelligence
- o Cognitive Science
- o IEEE Transactions on Pattern Analysis and Machine Intelligence
- o Foundations and Trends in Machine Learning
- o Journal of Memory and Language
- o Cognitive Psychology
- o Neural Networks
- o IEEE Transactions on Neural Networks and Learning Systems
- o IEEE Intelligent Systems
- o Knowledge-based Systems

GUIDE TO USING THE CHAPTERS

For each of the chapters, I provide next some various ways to use the chapter material. You can assign the tasks as individual homework assignments, or the tasks can be used with team projects for the class. You can easily layout a series of assignments, such as indicating that the students are to do item "a" below for say Chapter 1, then "b" for the next chapter of the book, and so on.

a) What is the main point of the chapter and describe in your own words the significance of the topic,

b) Identify at least two aspects in the chapter that you agree with, and support your concurrence by providing at least one other outside researched item as support; make sure to explain your basis for disagreeing with the aspects,

c) Identify at least two aspects in the chapter that you disagree with, and support your disagreement by providing at least one other outside researched item as support; make sure to explain your basis for disagreeing with the aspects,

d) Find an aspect that was not covered in the chapter, doing so by conducting outside research, and then explain how that aspect ties into the chapter and what significance it brings to the topic,

e) Interview a specialist in industry about the topic of the chapter, collect from them their thoughts and opinions, and readdress the chapter by citing your source and how they compared and contrasted to the material,

f) Interview a relevant academic professor or researcher in a college or university about the topic of the chapter, collect from them their thoughts and opinions, and readdress the chapter by citing your source and how they compared and contrasted to the material,

g) Try to update a chapter by finding out the latest on the topic, and ascertain whether the issue or topic has now been solved or whether it is still being addressed, explain what you come up with.

The above are all ways in which you can get the students of your class involved in considering the material of a given chapter. You could mix things up by having one of those above assignments per each week, covering the chapters over the course of the semester or quarter.

As a reminder, here are the chapters of the book and you can select whichever chapters you find most valued for your particular class:

<u>Chapter Title</u>

Lance B. Eliot

Companion Book By This Author

Advances in AI and Autonomous Vehicles: Cybernetic Self-Driving Cars

Practical Advances in Artificial Intelligence (AI) and Machine Learning

by

Dr. Lance B. Eliot, MBA, PhD

This title is available via Amazon and other book sellers

Lance B. Eliot

Companion Book By This Author

Self-Driving Cars:
"The Mother of All AI Projects"

by Dr. Lance B. Eliot, MBA, PhD

This title is available via Amazon and other book sellers

Companion Book By This Author

Innovation and Thought Leadership on Self-Driving Driverless Cars

by Dr. Lance B. Eliot, MBA, PhD

This title is available via Amazon and other book sellers

Lance B. Eliot

Companion Book By This Author

New Advances in AI Autonomous Driverless Cars Self-Driving Cars

by Dr. Lance B. Eliot, MBA, PhD

This title is available via Amazon and other book sellers

Companion Book By This Author

Introduction to
Driverless Self-Driving Cars

by Dr. Lance B. Eliot, MBA, PhD

This title is available via Amazon and other book sellers

Companion Book By This Author

Autonomous Vehicle Driverless Self-Driving Cars and Artificial Intelligence

by Dr. Lance B. Eliot, MBA, PhD

Chapter Title

This title is available via Amazon and other book sellers

Companion Book By This Author

Transformative Artificial Intelligence Driverless Self-Driving Cars

by Dr. Lance B. Eliot, MBA, PhD

Chapter Title

1 Eliot Framework for AI Self-Driving Cars

2 Kinetosis Anti-Motion Sickness for Self-Driving Cars

3 Rain Driving for Self-Driving Cars

4 Edge Computing for Self-Driving Cars

5 Motorcycles as AI Self-Driving Vehicles

6 CAPTCHA Cyber-Hacking and Self-Driving Cars

7 Probabilistic Reasoning for Self-Driving Cars

8 Proving Grounds for Self-Driving Cars

9 Frankenstein and AI Self-Driving Cars

10 Omnipresence for Self-Driving Cars

11 Looking Behind You for Self-Driving Cars

12 Over-The-Air (OTA) Updating for Self-Driving Cars

13 Snow Driving for Self-Driving Cars

14 Human-Aided Training for Self-Driving Cars

15 Privacy for Self-Driving Cars

16 Transduction Vulnerabilities for Self-Driving Cars

17 Conversations Computing and Self-Driving Cars

18 Flying Debris and Self-Driving Cars

19 Citizen AI for Self-Driving Cars

This title is available via Amazon and other book sellers

Companion Book By This Author
Disruptive Artificial Intelligence and Driverless Self-Driving Cars
by Dr. Lance B. Eliot, MBA, PhD

Chapter Title

This title is available via Amazon and other book sellers

Companion Book By This Author

State-of-the-Art
AI Driverless Self-Driving Cars

by Dr. Lance B. Eliot, MBA, PhD

This title is available via Amazon and other book sellers

Lance B. Eliot

ABOUT THE AUTHOR

Dr. Lance B. Eliot, MBA, PhD is the CEO of Techbruim, Inc. and Executive Director of the Cybernetic Self-Driving Car Institute, and has over twenty years of industry experience including serving as a corporate officer in a billion dollar firm and was a partner in a major executive services firm. He is also a serial entrepreneur having founded, ran, and sold several high-tech related businesses. He previously hosted the popular radio show *Technotrends* that was also available on American Airlines flights via their in-flight audio program. Author or co-author of a dozen books and over 400 articles, he has made appearances on CNN, and has been a frequent speaker at industry conferences.

A former professor at the University of Southern California (USC), he founded and led an innovative research lab on Artificial Intelligence in Business. Known as the "AI Insider" his writings on AI advances and trends has been widely read and cited. He also previously served on the faculty of the University of California Los Angeles (UCLA), and was a visiting professor at other major universities. He was elected to the International Board of the Society for Information Management (SIM), a prestigious association of over 3,000 high-tech executives worldwide.

He has performed extensive community service, including serving as Senior Science Adviser to the Vice Chair of the Congressional Committee on Science & Technology. He has served on the Board of the OC Science & Engineering Fair (OCSEF), where he is also has been a Grand Sweepstakes judge, and likewise served as a judge for the Intel International SEF (ISEF). He served as the Vice Chair of the Association for Computing Machinery (ACM) Chapter, a prestigious association of computer scientists. Dr. Eliot has been a shark tank judge for the USC Mark Stevens Center for Innovation on start-up pitch competitions, and served as a mentor for several incubators and accelerators in Silicon Valley and Silicon Beach. He served on several Boards and Committees at USC, including having served on the Marshall Alumni Association (MAA) Board in Southern California.

Dr. Eliot holds a PhD from USC, MBA, and Bachelor's in Computer Science, and earned the CDP, CCP, CSP, CDE, and CISA certifications. Born and raised in Southern California, and having traveled and lived internationally, he enjoys scuba diving, surfing, and sailing.

ADDENDUM

Top Trends in
AI Self-Driving Cars

Practical Advances in Artificial Intelligence (AI)
and Machine Learning

By

Dr. Lance B. Eliot, MBA, PhD

———

For supplemental materials of this book, visit:

www.ai-selfdriving-cars.guru

For special orders of this book, contact:

LBE Press Publishing

Email: LBE.Press.Publishing@gmail.com

www.ingramcontent.com/pod-product-compliance
Lightning Source LLC
Chambersburg PA
CBHW051232050326
40689CB00007B/889